Praise for Staying with the Catholic Church

The parable of the wheat and the weeds—Christ's warning in Matthew 13:24–30 that his Church will always be home to both great saints and great sinners—is an especially apt one for this Catholic moment. David Bonagura makes a powerful case for listening to the Lord, remaining within the Body of Christ, working for the Church's purification, and getting on with the New Evangelization.

George Weigel | Distinguished Senior Fellow and
William E. Simon Chair in Catholic Studies
Ethics and Public Policy Center

At a time when the Catholic Church is suffering from declining membership, parishes and schools closing, and the revelation of clerical sexual abuse and cover-ups by Church authorities, many people want to know why they should remain faithful to the Church. David Bonagura has given us a well-written, easy to read guide with this simple and life-changing answer: The Church is where we meet Christ. Faithfulness to Him in His Church is what Christ asks of every one of his followers.

Father Gerald E. Murray, J.C.D. | Pastor,
Holy Family Church, New York City

One of the major challenges for Catholics today is maintaining their commitment to the objective truths of the Catholic Church in a world filled with skepticism. When the failures of some in the hierarchy catch the attention of the media there can be a temptation to view the Church as a purely human institution no different from any other organization. This can easily lead to discouragement and the erosion of belief. David Bonagura honestly acknowledges the failings of Church leaders and Catholics in history while at the same time focusing on the divine foundations of the Church that call us to remain faithful to the mission of the Catholic Church and her Founder, Jesus Christ. Bonagura has challenged us to deepen our commitment to the spiritual treasures that the Church generously shares with us through Sacred Scripture, Sacred Tradition, the Creed, the Sacraments, Catholic moral teaching, and the witness of the saints and mystics throughout the Church's history. Bonagura's timely and readable book, Staying with the Catholic Church, will be a blessing for anyone who wishes to understand why many Catholics still love their Church and remain faithful to the Splendor of Truth that the Church teaches, leading them to holiness and eternal life.

Bishop John O. Barres, S.T.D., J.C.L.
Diocese of Rockville Centre

David Bonagura has put his finger on a particularly sore spot in the Church today. Not only our fellow believers, but even some of our leaders at the highest levels sound an uncertain trumpet, over and beyond the loss of moral authority caused by the abuse crisis. In simple, clear language—the kind of straight talk we need at a moment like this—he explains both why we should never abandon Christ's own Church, his vehicle of salvation, and how we can each stay faithful despite the many challenges all around us at present.

Robert Royal, Ph.D. | President, Faith and Reason Institute

STAYING WITH THE CATHOLIC CHURCH

STAYING WITH THE CATHOLIC CHURCH

Trusting God's Plan of Salvation

David G. Bonagura, Jr.

Scepter

DEDICATION

To Joe, Charlie, Stephen, Anthony, Maggie, and John

Nihil obstat:
Reverend Walter F. Kedjierski, Ph.D., *Censor deputatus*

Imprimatur:
Most Reverend John O. Barres, S.T.D., *Bishop of Rockville Centre*
November 11, 2020

Published by Scepter Publishers, Inc.
info@scepterpublishers.org
www.scepterpublishers.org
800-322-8773
New York

Cover design by Rose Design
Page design and pagination by Rose Design

Library of Congress Control Number: 2020948294

ISBN: 9781594174094 (pbk.)
ISBN: 9781594174124 (eBook)

Printed in the United States of America

CONTENTS

The Universe is a single body (thanks Galileo)

ACKNOWLEDGMENTS

St. Paul speaks of the Church as a single body of many members, all of whom play essential, albeit different, roles in fulfilling God's will. Similarly, this book has come to be thanks to the generous help of many friends, who have each contributed in some way to its writing.

My thanks first go to Fr. Dennis Suglia, who put me into contact with Mr. Ralph Areste. Ralph and I spent many enjoyable hours together discussing the present needs of the Church and how best to address them. With his help, the idea for this book was conceived. Ralph patiently read each chapter as it appeared, offering suggestions and identifying what needed better explanation. I am grateful for his wisdom and for his friendship.

My colleagues at St. Joseph's Seminary were tremendously generous in tracking down resources. My sincere thanks goes to Fr. Solanus Benfatti, CFR, who aided my research into St. Francis of Assisi that appears in these pages, as well as to the wonderful library staff of Connor Flatz, Jim Monti, and Barbara Kelly. I also was able to borrow books from Fr. Christopher Sullivan, who was my family's unofficial chaplain while he was assigned to our parish.

Before a chapter was passed to Ralph, my former colleague and dear friend, Mr. Kevin Dugal, enthusiastically volunteered to be my first reader. Kevin kindly identified the manuscript's weaknesses and offered suggestions to sharpen my prose.

Ralph also introduced me to the hardworking staff at Scepter Publishers, Bob Singerline, John Powers, and Meredith Koopman. I am extraordinarily grateful for Bob's support for this project, and for John and Meredith's scrupulous editing of the manuscript. This is a much better book thanks to their sharp eyes. Any errors that remain are my own.

At my core, I am a teacher who writes, not a writer who happens to teach. I remain ever grateful to the wonderful Catholic institutions with which I have been associated over the years. In no particular order, I would like to thank Bishop James Massa, Fr. Peter Vaccari, Fr. Kevin O'Reilly, and Dr. Donna Eschenauer of St. Joseph's Seminary; Dr. Marianne Mount, Dr. Peter Brown, Dr. Marie Nuar, and Mrs. Judy Welsh of Catholic Distance University; Fr. Daniel Lahart, SJ, and Fr. Anthony Andreassi, CO, of Regis High School;

and Br. Kenneth Hoagland, SM, of Kellenberg Memorial High School.

The foundation of Catholic life is the local parish, which brings the Church to life for each of us. I offer my sincere thanks to my pastor, Fr. Thomas Fusco of Our Lady of Victory Church, for his tireless efforts in caring for the souls of my family and my community.

Lastly, my deepest gratitude goes to my wife and best friend, Amanda, for her constant love and support for everything I do.

Hannity (FOX NEWS) went to Pius Prep Sem

PREFACE

Throughout her history, the Catholic Church's credibility as the vessel of God's grace has been undermined not just by her human members, but by her own leaders whose office it is to explain and exemplify Jesus Christ's divine teachings. In our own day, we have learned that some priests preyed upon and abused young people, and that some bishops, who were supposed to be fostering their people's spiritual growth, then covered up these horrific sins. For believers and nonbelievers alike, these events have become, in the original meaning of the word, a horrific scandal—a "stumbling block" to faith and belief.

This book attempts to help believers to move beyond this stumbling block. In no way does it seek to hide or defend the sins committed by the Church's members and leaders, but instead to understand the Church and to see why she is worthy of continued faith and support. It aims to show why we should stay with the Catholic Church.

Since God designed the world so that nature and other human beings might lead us to the divine, and since currently it is human sins that are obscuring the divine from us, this book will proceed by addressing the most pressing questions concerning the Church by recasting them in light of their eternal, divine significance. After all, the Church does not exist of human initiative, nor are her objectives merely temporal. Rather, founded by divine initiative, the Church exists to meet a supernatural goal that lies beyond the limits of human sight. Only when we consider the true nature of the Church do we find the reasons to remain with her.

If we can have faith in the God whom we cannot see, perhaps we can also have faith that we can encounter God through the Church that we can see, even as some members' sins obstruct our sight. For Jesus Christ

> is before all things, and in him all things hold together. He is the head of the body, the Church; he is the beginning, the first-born from the dead, that in everything he might be pre-eminent. For in him the fullness of God was pleased to dwell, and through him to reconcile to himself all things, whether on earth or in heaven, making peace by the blood of his cross. (Col 1:17–20)

To how this body, the Church, exists in relation to its head, Christ the fullness of God, we will now turn.

INTRODUCTION

ROCKING THE BOAT

Imagine what Peter must have been thinking.

He had been the designated leader of a new movement taking the Jewish world by storm. His master was working unthinkable signs among the people; he restored sight to the blind and strength to the lame. He mysteriously multiplied some bread and fish to feed a crowd of thousands. He even raised people from the dead.

And then something went terribly wrong.

Suddenly, armed guards seized the master, tortured him, subjected him to a sham trial, and then brutally crucified him. Offering nothing by way of resistance, the master submitted himself to his captors' insults and beatings, opening not his mouth. He died naked on a cross, abandoned by his closest friends. Including by Peter.

What could Peter have been thinking the following day, as the lacerated body of his master, Jesus of Nazareth, lay cold in a tomb? Rather than fight to save Jesus, Peter denied that he even knew him—not once, not twice, but on three separate occasions. He was supposed to be the rock, yet he was shaken to his core. And he had no one to blame but himself.

The next morning, everything changed. The tomb was empty. Jesus shocked the world by rising from the dead. Immediately, the risen Lord gave new life to Peter. He did not forget the betrayal; instead he helped Peter reverse it. "Simon, son of John, do you love me more than these?"

Even though he had failed Jesus when it counted most, Peter was given a new opportunity to be the rock of the risen Lord's kingdom. Only now he understood that he had not been given the keys to an earthly kingdom, but to the kingdom of heaven.

Peter went to work right away. As we will see later, on the morning of Pentecost he proclaimed the world's first homily as he explained who Jesus is and what we must do to be saved. Along with his brother apostles, Peter spread the gospel of Jesus Christ throughout Jerusalem and then beyond. Like Jesus, he even healed a lame man and raised a woman from the dead, except he acted not by his own power, but by the name of Jesus of Nazareth.

Yet Peter did not always do the right thing. When he sailed to Antioch, he withdrew from the same Gentiles who he had said were authentic Christians and, instead, associated only with Jewish Christians. For this, he drew rebuke from Paul, who was also in the city with him. Paul did not challenge Peter's authority, but his ill-considered behavior, and urged him to act according to his earlier decree in Jerusalem. Christ made Peter the rock and bestowed upon him special gifts to serve as the leader of his flock and chief teacher of his gospel. Of the gifts he received, perfection was not among them.

The story of Peter is the story of the Church throughout the ages—acts of fidelity, proclamations of faith, and glimmers of heroism mixed unevenly with sin, quarreling, and betrayal. One of the Church's nicknames is the barque of Peter, and for good reason. Not only is Peter the Church's captain, but his life is synonymous with that of the Church he was asked to lead—sailing a crooked path to Christ, constantly buffered by external threats and internal unrest. Though sometimes listless or even leaking, the boat that is the Church has never sunk, for she has the gospel as her map and Jesus Christ as her magnetic north, even if those on the boat sometimes fail to read the compass correctly.

At his death, Peter passed his authority as bishop of Rome and leader of the Church universal on to Linus, his successor, who, like Peter before him, died a martyr's death. Linus then passed on his authority in the same manner, so that the Pope, the head of the Catholic Church, is called the successor of St. Peter. Like Peter, some popes have betrayed the master's trust, and more than once. And, like Peter, their legitimacy depends not on their personal merits, but on Jesus Christ who constituted his Church on a human rock, and on his successors.

Among the successors of St. Peter are courageous and holy men. Pope Leo the Great (r. 440–461) was a dutiful pastor, regularly preaching the gospel even as he quelled eastern heresies. He boldly confronted Attila the Hun, and convinced him to turn back rather than attack Rome. Pope Gregory the Great (r. 590–604), born into a wealthy aristocratic family, renounced his wealth and high position in Rome's civic government to become a monk. His devout prayer life and asceticism drew the admiration of many, who elected him pope against his will. He energetically governed the Church with this same monastic spirit, living up to the title he gave himself: servant of the servants of God. He sponsored missionaries to evangelize the fringes of Europe, including England, then under continual pagan invasion; built monasteries; enforced rules for clergy and bishops; and helped codify the Mass and liturgical music. Pope Pius V (r. 1566–1572) zealously implemented the reforms of the Council of Trent and conducted his pontificate in the same austere manner that he had been living before his election. He published a catechism that responded to Protestant heresies, and he updated the Roman Missal used at Mass. When he organized a coalition of nations to repel a Turkish invasion of Europe, he implored all of Christendom to pray the Rosary for victory, which he attributed to Mary's intercession despite the odds against the Christians. Because of Pius' holy life, popes to this day wear a white cassock in his honor.

These three successors of Peter faithfully navigated the Church toward her proper destiny. Yet others have rocked the boat in ways that beggar belief. Less than 200 years after St. Peter's death, Hippolytus became the Church's first "antipope," a leader of a schismatic group that denounced the real pope as a fraud; he lasted as a rival claimant to the real pope for eighteen years. Sadly, over the centuries there would be several antipopes after him, all of whom, in refusing to accept the legitimate pope's authority, introduced deadly division into the Body of Christ. Honorius I (r. 625–638) wrote sloppily about the divinity of Christ in a private letter, and then was posthumously condemned for heresy. Pope Formosus (r. 891–896) was a conscientious leader, but his successor Stephen VI, motivated by political alliances, so detested him that he put Formosus' decomposing corpse on trial. He declared Formosus guilty of perjury and other crimes, ordered his three fingers used for blessings cut off, and had his body thrown into the Tiber River. If we turn to the moral failures of popes, the list of vicars of Christ who were anything but Christ-like, awash in political corruption, ruthless calculations, mistresses, and illegitimate children, is as long as it is nauseating.

What binds together the saints and scoundrels who served as the successors of St. Peter? And what kept the Church from capsizing, fading into the dustbin of history along with countless other empires and ruling dynasties that were once temporally more powerful? The answer is Jesus Christ, who, through the Holy Spirit, guarantees the Church's legitimacy as the fount of his grace and teaching by working through the channels he has willed.

The Church's structures, offices, and ruling authorities are necessary to keep Christ present in the world, but his presence transcends their limitations—including the moral failures of his own vicars. Christ, being God, knew his vicars would fail him, as he knew St. Peter would. That did not keep him from establishing the Church or entrusting St. Peter with the keys to the kingdom of heaven. Knowing human weaknesses, Christ engineered the Church so that she would never fail to deliver his salvation to the world. Immediately after declaring Peter the rock of the Church, Christ added this: "The gates of Hades shall not prevail against it" (Mt 16:19). That the Church still stands today, despite all the horrible sins of

her members—popes, bishops, priests, and lay people—
is the ultimate proof of Christ's promise.

In Peter's life, we see that Jesus Christ has endowed
his Church with a mission that will continue until the
end of time. This book explores this mission in detail.
We will see what the Church is and why Christ founded
her the way that he did, with sacraments, a hierarchy,
and a body of teaching. We will also see why we need
the Church, and what our role is within her. By knowing
her mission and constitution, we hope to learn to love
the Church, not by overlooking her members' sins, but
by coming to know her as our loving mother who wants
nothing more than to fulfill her mission: to lead us to
Christ's salvation.

Love's

pygmalian
woman in his image

1

What is the Church?

Faith is integral to the human experience. It is an act of trust in another person, and we see it from the earliest ages in children, who learn by unconsciously imitating their parents as they absorb behaviors and social cues. As they age, they attend school, where they learn about the world and how it functions through essential links in the learning process: teachers.

Teachers serve as a bridge between students and the knowledge they seek, and teachers can only be successful if they have the trust of their students. If students harbor animus against the teacher, or if they think the teacher is incompetent, their learning will be minimal, however important or interesting the subject matter may be. The opposite is also the case: students who really like their teacher are more inclined to the subject matter as well. So often students will say that their love for literature or chemistry was inspired not merely by books and equations, but by their teacher who made the subject matter come alive. When students like a teacher, they implicitly trust her as a person and as an authority in her field.

Knowledge of Jesus Christ comes to us in the same way. We do not encounter him on our own, but through other people. For most Catholics, parents and siblings are the initial bridges that connect us to Christ, and they first do so by asking the Church to have us baptized. As we age, we encounter more people who also serve as bridges to Christ: our parish priests, our religious education teachers, saints, and other religious leaders about whom we read or see through visual media. Like students in school, we have to trust these bridges, these teachers of the Faith, if we are to accept their message. So often our understanding of Christ is influenced, for better or for worse, by the quality of the lessons we receive from these teachers.

In connecting us to Christ, these human bridges are essential agents of faith, which, as St. Paul teaches, "comes by what is heard, and what is heard comes by the preaching of Christ" (Romans 10:17). There cannot be faith if there is no one to preach Christ and his gospel to others. The apostles, as the first preachers of the gospel, are our bridges to Christ. Their teachings and writings form the foundation for all those who have ever professed their faith in Christ so that all believers have been brought together into a single body that we call the Church, which is the people of God united together as the Body of Christ.

If we consider the four nouns in our definition of the Church—people, God, body, Christ—we see that the Church is comprised of both natural and supernatural elements. People, of course, are the principal natural element, as it is they to whom God has revealed himself and through whom the Church's divine elements are channeled. God's revelation is not an object to be discovered, like a dinosaur fossil, but a living truth that finds its expression in the hearts and minds of the Church's human members.[1]

The great German theologian Romano Guardini clarifies that "the people" does not refer to the masses or to the uncultured. By contrast, "the people" means

> the primary association of those human beings who by race, country, and historical antecedents share the same life and destiny. The people is a human society which maintains an unbroken continuity with the roots of nature and life and obeys their intrinsic laws. The people contains—not numerically or quantitatively, but in essential quality—the whole of

1. For this understanding of revelation, see Joseph Ratzinger, *Milestones: Memoirs 1927–1977*, trans. Erasmo Leiva-Merikakis (San Francisco: Ignatius Press, 1998), 127; and Joseph Ratzinger, "The Question of the Concept of Tradition: A Provisional Response." *God's Word: Scripture, Tradition, Office*, ed. Peter Hünermann and Thomas Söding, trans. Henry Taylor (San Francisco: Ignatius Press, 2008), 41–89.

> mankind, in all its human variety of ages, sexes, temperament, mental, and physical condition.[2]

The people of God, transcending the limits of time, race, and country, is, on the human level, an association that shares the entire history contained in the Old and New Testaments, the teachings of Christ handed on by the Catholic Church, and the destiny of eternal life with God that is promised after death.

Body is the second natural element in our definition, and it teaches us that the people in the Church, in addition to sharing a common history, law, and destiny, are united as one entity. What unites them above all is the shared content of their belief—the creed—that they have received through the unbroken chain of witnesses that extends back to the apostles and to Jesus.

This creed proclaims a deeper unity for this body, which springs from a real event that all members must undergo: baptism, through which people are *incorporated*, or "brought into the body." St. Paul explains that by the power of the Holy Spirit, baptism incorporates us into Christ's body:

> For just as the body is one and has many members, and all the members of the body, though many, are

---

2. Romano Guardini, *The Meaning of the Church*, trans. Ada Lane (Providence: Cluny Media, 2018), 10–11.

> one body, so it is with Christ. For by one Spirit we were all baptized into one body—Jews or Greeks, slaves or free—and all were made to drink of one Spirit. (1 Cor 12:12–13)

The two supernatural elements of our definition lead directly to the mystery of the holy Trinity. The people who are members of the Church are not autonomous; they are not even a people of their own enterprise. They are the people *of God*, who himself is the very purpose for their association. The people belong to God because he called them: our membership comes from his initiative, not ours. Our bridge analogy makes this clear: none of us has come to God through our own powers, but through others who have brought us to him and poured the waters of baptism upon us. Etymologically, the word "church" comes from the Greek *kyriakon*, meaning "of the Lord." "Church" is the English word that translates St. Paul's "*ecclesia*," meaning "the assembly of those called out." Those who are called out to join the assembly are invited by the Lord according to his will.

The people of God are directed toward a particular person: they are incorporated into the Body *of Christ*. Christ is the ultimate revelation of God to the world, as Christ is the Word, the eternal thought of God the Father. Through the Incarnation of the Son of God as the man Jesus Christ, God shows us definitively that we, his people, are loved unconditionally, and we are to show our thanks by loving him and loving one another. This love, Christ shows us, is not one of mere sentiment, but one of willing self-sacrifice for another: "This is my commandment, that you love one another as I have loved you. Greater love has no man than this, that a man lay down his life for his friends" (Jn 15:12–13).

Pope Pius XII provides a vivid analogy for understanding the mysterious way in which Christ aids his Church:

> As the nerves extend from the head to all parts of the human body and give them power to feel and to move, in like manner our Savior communicates strength and power to his Church so that the things of God are understood more clearly and are more eagerly desired by the faithful. From him streams into the body of the Church all the light with which those who believe are divinely illumined, and all the grace by which they are made holy as he is holy.[3]

The Church, then, is the mystical Body of Christ—mystical because of the supernatural way in which Christ unites the faithful to himself. Through this profound union, the Church extends and perpetuates the Incarnation of God's Son in time. This is a staggering claim:

3. Pius XII, Encyclical on the Mystical Body of Christ *Mystici Corporis Christi* (June 29, 1943), 49. Vatican website: *www.vatican.va.*

that the Church continues the real presence of Jesus Christ, born 2,000 years ago in Bethlehem, all over the world today. St. Paul calls Christ "the image of the invisible God" (Col 1:15). In a like manner, the Church is the image of the invisible Christ, who now reigns with God the Father for all eternity, yet he is still present among us in the Church through the power of the Holy Spirit. When we come to the Church, we come to Christ.

In considering Church history, though, how can this body claim that it not only exists in the name of Christ, but is, in fact, inseparably and invisibly connected to him? Too often her members seek not divine grace and eternal salvation, but their own self-aggrandizement. Such behavior obscures the Church's divine elements, and makes this people seem to belong to anything but God.

It takes faith to believe that the man Jesus is really the Son of God. Scientific tests cannot certify his divinity. Jesus' miracles do not coerce belief. Many of Jesus' contemporaries witnessed his inexplicable healings and other wondrous deeds, yet they refused to believe. They doubted that such a mighty prophet could be the son of a carpenter and hail from Nazareth. Seeing does not guarantee belief, which follows from God's grace and from our own inference: for Jesus to say and do what he did, he *had to be God.*

Likewise, it takes faith to believe that the Church is really the people of God united as the Body of Christ.

Science also cannot ascertain this claim. And, if anything, the sins of Church members undermine it. Is it possible, then, to make the inference about the Church's direct connection to Christ in the way that we make the inference about Jesus being God? Next to the terrible list of sins, we also must consider an equally long list of wondrous deeds performed by Church members, deeds performed explicitly in the name of Jesus. The apostles cured the sick wherever they traveled. St. Francis of Assisi inexplicably received the stigmata, the same wounds that Jesus had, which bled and inflicted pain for the final two years of his life. St. John Vianney read the souls of people he had never met in the confessional. St. Pio of Pietrelcina, who also bore the stigmata, but for fifty years, is attributed the curious recovery from a coma of a woman he visited in 1921.

These are only a few of the most miraculous deeds performed by saints within their lifetimes. Thousands more such deeds are attributed to deceased saints interceding before God on behalf of men and women imploring their assistance on earth. To these have been granted healings from incurable illnesses, the birth of children in seemingly impossible situations, and the recovery of people injured in life-threatening accidents. In these miraculous healings, we see the fullness of the Church at work: living members of the Church seek the help of those exemplary members who have gone before them. We call this union of the baptized that transcends the limits of time the communion of saints, which we affirm each Sunday at Mass when we recite the Creed.

Not all of us get to experience miracles and healings firsthand. But all Catholics are beneficiaries of tremendous and even heroic works by saints of the Church. From the Church's earliest days through today, charitable works have been established to care for the sick and dying, to educate children, to help the poor, to lead people to heaven. So often the founder of these works that have now spread all over the world is a canonized saint. Some of these saints are well known and others less so: St. Jerome Emiliani established houses to care for orphans in multiple cities; St. Camillus de Lellis founded an order of priests to care for the sick; St. John Bosco established a religious order dedicated to teaching and caring for poor city boys; St. Jeanne Jugan founded the Little Sisters of the Poor to care for the elderly who have no one to care for them; St. Josemaría Escrivá founded Opus Dei to aid Catholics in living God's call to holiness within ordinary life; St. Theresa of Calcutta founded the Missionaries of Charity to bring Christ's love to the poorest of the poor in India's slums.

What each one of these saints, and the countless others not mentioned, has in common, regardless of the specific work accomplished, is that each was motivated by an incredible love of God that spilled over into a love of other people, often men and women who were unknown to them and who lived on the margins of society.

We may not get to meet canonized saints within our lifetimes, but each of us can think of men and women from our families, parishes, workplaces, and neighborhoods who are inspirations to us by their dedication to prayer, to the service of the Church and to the parish, and to other people. These men and women live saintly lives by loving God, obeying his divine will, and by loyally serving their fellow human beings. None of them are perfect or without sin, but all of them are animated by God at the core of their being. Their fame will never transcend their neighborhoods, but they are witnesses of the very purpose of the Church: handing on the salvation of Jesus Christ to all people.

As mentioned, the miracles performed by Christ did not, and cannot, coerce belief. Similarly, the great works of the saints, both famous and anonymous, do not, and cannot, coerce belief that Christ is truly connected to his Church as her head, that there are divine elements within her, and that divine life is dispensed through her. To believe that the Church possesses real divine elements also requires an act of faith on our part. We trust that God is present in the Church and guiding her, even if there are many appearances to the contrary.

The Church's Divine Elements

Each Sunday at Mass, we stand to profess our Faith as Catholics. Near the end of this profession, we say, "I believe in one, holy, catholic, and apostolic Church." These four adjectives are divine gifts that God has bestowed on the Church; we call them the four marks. How do we know that the Church possesses these marks? When we look at Scripture's description of the primitive Church in her first days of existence, we see that these four properties were present in the Church at the very start:

> So those who received [Peter's] word were baptized, and there were added that day about three thousand souls. And they devoted themselves to the apostles' teaching and fellowship, to the breaking of bread and the prayers. And fear came upon every soul; and many wonders and signs were done through the apostles. And all who believed were together and had all things in common; and they sold their possessions and goods and distributed them to all, as any had need. And day by day, attending the temple together and breaking bread in their homes, they partook of

> food with glad and generous hearts, praising God and having favor with all the people. (Acts 2:41–47)

We see oneness in three thousand souls becoming a single body through baptism; their shared belief then brought them together in fellowship. We see holiness in the celebration of the sacraments, particularly baptism and the "breaking of bread," the Eucharist, as well as in their prayer and attendance in the temple to praise God. We see catholicity, or universality, in the increasing number of believers, and in the distribution of their goods to everyone. And we see apostolicity in the fidelity shown to the apostles' teaching and in the mighty deeds they performed in the name of Christ. 2,000 years later, these marks endure, even when human frailty and sin injure the Church. We will examine each of the four marks individually.

The Church is one because she is one body, with one divine founder who entrusted his singular teachings to her. From the first group of apostles in Jerusalem, faith in Jesus Christ spread gradually from region to region, sometimes with ease and sometimes with tremendous hardships, including the violent slaying of missionary preachers. Today the countless parishes, church buildings, chapels, shrines, and Catholic schools spread throughout the world are all united, as they are all physical manifestations of the spiritual union that, transcending geographical and ethnic limits, Catholics share through baptism. Should we enter any one of them during the celebration of the Mass, we see the ultimate expression of our unity: an entire group of believers gathered around the altar to participate in the re-presentation of Christ's saving sacrifice on the Cross.

Sin strikes directly against the Church's oneness, as it wrongly elevates the self at the expense of the body. By violating the laws of Christ, each sin wounds him and his body by turning believer against believer. Sins against the Church's oneness include Catholic leaders and theologians who teach their own doctrine rather than that of the Church, and individual Catholics who think they do not need to attend Mass on Sunday. Christ prophesized the effect that an attack on him has on his disciples, quoting the prophet Zechariah: "I will strike the shepherd, and the sheep of the flock will be scattered" (Mt 26:31).

But the sins of individuals cannot destroy the oneness of the Church, for nothing can separate Christ the head from his body the Church. God promises the sinner that "I will not remove from him my merciful love, or be false to my faithfulness. I will not violate my covenant, or alter the word that went forth from my lips" (Psalm 89:33–34). Just as we have to make an act of faith that God is present in the Church when we see the good works she performs, we have to make an even deeper act of faith that God maintains the integrity of the Church even when some members of the body behave as if they had separated themselves from it.

The mark of catholicity is related to the oneness of the Church. The Church is catholic, or universal, in two senses: first, because Christ is fully present to her; and, second, because the teachings of Christ that she exists to transmit are valid for the whole world.[4] Regarding the first, St. Ignatius of Antioch, writing at the end of the first century, expresses the mystery of Christ's enduring presence in the Church in a profoundly simple manner: "[W]herever Christ Jesus is, there is the Catholic Church."[5]

The second sense of the Church's catholicity concerns the Church's mission as her divine founder directly commanded:

> Go therefore and make disciples of all nations, baptizing them in the name of the Father and of the Son and of the Holy Spirit, teaching them to observe all that I have commanded you. (Mt 28:19–20)

All people, regardless of birthplace, nationality, or culture, are equally capable of receiving the Church's teachings

---

4. *Catechism of the Catholic Church,* 2nd ed. (Washington, DC: Libreria Editrice Vaticana—United States Conference of Catholic Bishops, 2000), (hereafter *CCC*) 830.

5. Ignatius of Antioch, *Epistle to the Smyrnaeans*, 8. Translation by the author. Cf. *CCC*, 830.

about Christ and his saving message because Christ is the *Word* of God. By his very nature, he speaks to us in a way we all can understand.

Sins against catholicity, particularly the breaking away from the structure of the Church to establish an autonomous Christian community, do not diminish the Church's universality, and neither does the absence of the Church from certain parts of the world. In both cases, human weakness and limitation have inhibited the preaching of Christ through the Church to one degree or another. Christ remains the same, yesterday, today, and forever, and human beings remain equally capable of receiving him and the Church that bears his name should they have the desire, and the faith, to do so.

A third mark of the Church is apostolicity, that is, the foundation of the Church on the apostles, the original and essential bridges that connect us to Christ. Christ entrusted the apostles with his authority and he ordained them to serve as teachers, priests, and governors of his Church. From the apostles stem, in the words of the Second Vatican Council, "everything which contributes toward the holiness of life and increase in faith of the peoples of God," including the Church's teachings, laws, worship, practices, and way of life.[6]

6. Dogmatic Constitution on Divine Revelation, *Dei Verbum* (November 18, 1965), 8. Vatican website: *www.vatican.va.*

Bishops are the visible guarantee of the oneness and catholicity of the Church. At the start of the second century, St. Ignatius of Antioch set forth very clear instructions in this regard:

> All of you, follow your bishop, as Jesus Christ followed the Father . . . Let no one do anything pertaining to the Church without the bishop. Let that Eucharist be valid which is under the bishop or the one to whom he commits it. Wherever the bishop appears, there let the people be.[7]

Because of the unbroken succession of episcopal ordination, we know that the Church's Faith, sacraments, and laws are authentic. More will be said about the role of bishops in leading the Church in Chapter 4.

The fourth and final mark of the Church is holiness, and it is this one that causes so many questions today.

First, we have to consider what it means to be holy. Holiness is not synonymous with "perfect," which means complete, whole, lacking nothing. Only God is perfect. Rather, to be holy is to be consecrated for and wholly dedicated to God. The Church as an institution is holy in this sense: she was established by a divine founder to achieve a divine goal: leading all her members back

---

7. Ignatius of Antioch, *Epistle to the Smyrnaeans*, 8. Translation by the author.

to God at the end of this life. God has entrusted to the Church divine gifts—oneness, sanctity, catholicity, apostolicity, sacraments, laws, teachings, the abiding presence of Christ himself—for the purpose of sanctifying, and thereby saving, souls.

It is the Church's human members who sin. Cardinal Henri de Lubac articulates the mysterious interplay between the Church's divine and human elements: "At one and the same time the Church is without sin in herself and never without sin in her members."[8] To say this is not to make excuses on the Church's behalf; this is a real distinction built into the nature of the Church herself. The divine elements of the Church aid and sanctify her human members but do not remake them into new, perfect humans without sin. With the redemption wrought by Christ, God, for reasons known to him alone, chose to enthrone us in heaven, not to restore us to the Garden of Eden here on earth.[9] Since God made us in his image and likeness, we, like him, have free will, with which we can choose God—or reject him. Each sin is a choice to reject him, who, in one of the great mysteries of salvation, respects our choice. He calls us

8. Henri de Lubac, *The Splendor of the Church*, trans. Michael Mason (San Francisco: Ignatius Press, 1999), 116–117.

9. "An Ancient Homily on Holy Saturday," *Liturgy of the Hours*, Office of Readings, Holy Saturday.

to him and provides his grace to help us, but he never compels us.

The goal of Jesus' mission was to sanctify us, to make us holy so we can live in God for all eternity. He did this not with a magic wand while he sat aloof and isolated from the sins of his creatures. Rather, he willingly descended into the depths of human misery, subjecting himself to the worst suffering imaginable, so that by his wounds we would be healed.

Joseph Ratzinger calls this seemingly paradoxical meeting of God's sanctifying grace with human beings who desperately need to be sanctified the Church's "unholy holiness."

> [Christ] has drawn sin to himself, made it his lot, and so revealed what true "holiness" is: not separation, but union; not judgment, but redeeming love. Is the Church not simply the continuation of God's deliberate plunge into human wretchedness; is she not simply the continuation of Jesus' habit of sitting at table with sinners, of his mingling with the misery of sin to the point where he actually seems to sink under its weight. Is there not revealed in the unholy holiness of the Church, as opposed to man's expectation of purity, God's true holiness, which is love, love that does not keep its distance in a sort of aristocratic,

> untouchable purity but mixes with the dirt of the world, in order thus to overcome it? Can, therefore, the holiness of the Church be anything else but the bearing with one another that comes, of course, from the fact that all of us are borne up by Christ?[10]

The Church's plunge into human wretchedness requires that those sick with sin minister divine medicine to their fellow sinners with the hope of vanquishing sin. All the divine elements of the Church exist for this purpose. The lingering reality of sin, in the words of Romano Guardini, makes "tragedy an integral part of the Church's nature, rooted in her very essence" because "the dispenser of salvation is so intimately conjoined with human shortcomings."[11] The Church's mission, therefore, creates a tension within herself that requires believers to "have the courage to endure a state of permanent dissatisfaction. The more deeply a man realizes what God is, the loftier his vision of Christ and his kingdom, the more keenly will he suffer" from the wounds inflicted upon the Church by her members.[12]

---

10. Joseph Ratzinger, *Introduction to Christianity* (San Francisco: Ignatius Press, 2004), 342–343.

11. Guardini, *The Meaning of the Church*, 53, 52.

12. Guardini, *The Meaning of the Church*, 55.

This tension, continues Guardini, "is the profound sorrow which lives in the souls of all great Christians, beneath all the joyousness of a child of God."[13] So we are in no way wrong to be angered and distressed by the sins committed by our fellow Church members, including those committed by our priests and bishops. But we cannot allow our distraught emotions to triumph and prompt us to leave the Church. We must remember that

> Christ lives on in the Church, but Christ crucified. One might almost venture to suggest that the defects of the Church are his cross. . . . [The defects] are permitted to crucify our faith, so that we may sincerely seek God and our salvation, not ourselves.[14]

That is to say, the continued presence of sin in the Church reminds us that each one of us is wounded, like our Lord, who remains the head of his mystical body that suffers with him on the cross. The redemption of Christ passed on by the Church comes only when we persevere through Good Friday to Easter Sunday. The suffering Church offers us her divine medicine so that we, too, can be freed from sin and then be glorified like our risen Lord.

---

13. Guardini, *The Meaning of the Church*, 56.

14. Guardini, *The Meaning of the Church*, 56.

What, then, are we to do at this critical moment in the Church's history? Again, we turn to Guardini.

> We must, therefore, love the Church as she is. Only so do we truly love her. He alone genuinely loves his friend who loves him as he is, even when he condemns his faults and tries to reform them. In the same way we must accept the Church as she is, and maintain this attitude in everyday life. To be sure we must not let our vision of her failings become obscured . . . But we must always see through and beyond these defects her essential nature. We must be convinced of her indestructibility and at the same time resolved to do everything that lies in our power, each in his own way and to the extent of his responsibility, to bring her closer to her ideal. This is the Catholic attitude toward the Church.[15]

To have this faith in the Church we have to dig more deeply into her essence. To her founding and to her Founder's intentions for her we now turn.

---

15. Guardini, *The Meaning of the Church*, 57–58.

2

Do I Need the Church?

In recent decades people have been quitting organized religions, Catholicism among them, at an alarming rate.[1] Survey data indicate that, of those who no longer attend religious services, a third assert that they prefer to "practice their faith in other ways."[2] Those who see no need for religious services by extension see no need for religion or church at all.

Religious services are the most central aspects of any organized religion, and Catholicism is no exception. The Second Vatican Council called the Church's liturgy the "summit and source" of the whole Christian life. From the liturgy flow the essential graces of the seven sacraments that we need to be sanctified by God; and to the liturgy, which

---

1. Pew Forum, "America's Changing Religious Landscape," May 12, 2015, and "In U.S., Decline of Christianity Continues at Rapid Pace," October 17, 2019.

2. Pew Forum, "Why Americans Go (and Don't Go) to Religious Services," August 1, 2018.

is the perfect worship of God, all other aspects of Catholicism, from its dogmas to its moral laws, are directed.[3]

There are, then, two very different approaches to God today: through the Church, or through one's own preference. The latter manifests the radical individualism that dominates the modern age and that deifies the individual person as the sole arbiter of what is good, true, right, and beautiful in the universe. An infamous U.S. Supreme Court opinion candidly articulates this perspective: "At the heart of liberty is the right to define one's own concept of existence, of meaning, of the universe, and of the mystery of human life."[4]

Regardless of intention or circumstance, when a person decides to follow Jesus on his own, he ends up dictating to God how he wants to live and how he wants the world to be. He chooses his own mode of worship and prayer, and he decides what moral code he wants to follow. In this, he could adhere closely to what is written in the Bible, or he could follow certain ancient aspects of Christian teaching while rejecting others. Whatever

---

3. Constitution on the Sacred Liturgy, *Sacrosanctum Concilium* (December 4, 1963), 6, 9–10, and Dogmatic Constitution on the Church, *Lumen Gentium* (November 21, 1964), 11. Vatican website: *www.vatican.va.*

4. *Planned Parenthood of Southern PA vs. Casey*, 505 U.S. 833, 851 (1992).

the choice, in this situation the individual, and not the Church or his ancestors in the Faith, effectively anoints himself as pope of his church of one. He unwittingly flips the petition of the Our Father on its head: instead of "thy kingdom come, thy will be done, on earth as it is in heaven," the individual prays, "my kingdom come, my will be done, on earth so may it be in heaven."

Underlining this radical form of individualism is the modern understanding of freedom: in order to be the sole arbiter of what is good in the world, in order to be pope of one's own church, a person must be *free from* any external constraint on his ability to choose. He then has an infinitude of wants and choices at his disposal, with no criteria directing what he should use his freedom *for*.

Because many have unwittingly absorbed this perspective, the Church's role in the world is often misperceived. She is not seen as the means established by Christ to bring us to salvation, but as an oppressive institution that imposes outdated rules for living on her adherents.

For sure, we desire by nature freedom from constraints and other factors we deem hostile to us. Yet the choices we make and actions we perform on a regular basis, though done at our own initiative, still are limited by numerous factors, including by the freedom of other human beings. The adage that the right to swing one's fist ends at another's nose reminds us that freedom is not, of itself, absolute, even though contemporary rhetoric conceives freedom as such. In particular, our society advocates vociferously for sexual freedom: the freedom to have relations with whomever one wishes, and to limit the procreation of children by abortion, sterilization, or artificial means.

We see quickly that today's narrative of radical individualism and unbridled freedom is false because it is divorced from the reality of ordinary experience. We simply cannot exist happily as solitary popes of our own churches. We are made for relationships, for communion with other people, and our freedom to act is inherently directed, and properly limited, by these relationships. There must be, then, a truth that exists independent of human will to direct our moral behavior. Our own lived experiences—the internal reality of conscience, the feelings of joy or guilt that naturally follow our actions, the existence of moral standards that transcend time and cultures—point to a truth that is real, objective, and knowable.

Upon reflection, we discern through reason that a moral law is innate to the world based upon the nature and purpose of things. We call this the natural law. An ordered nature then points us to a creator God who designed this order so that his creatures may flourish. Then, as an aid to our reason, God revealed to us his divine law that perfectly complements the natural law. Although it requires freedom *from* external coercion as a prerequisite, the heart of freedom exists *for* something external to the individual. And that something is to love another person more than oneself.

We find a shining example of the Catholic view of freedom in St. Maximilian Kolbe, a Catholic priest who, though imprisoned in Auschwitz, was freer than any prison guard. Knowing that the Nazis could harm his body but could not touch his soul, Maximilian stepped forward and offered himself in place of a man whom the Nazis had sentenced to death. In dying as Christ did, Maximilian showed us how to live.

It follows, then, that in committing ourselves in faith to Jesus Christ, we are best served not by inventing our own religion, but in committing ourselves to Christ's body, the Church. Without the Church we become prisoners of our own limited powers. The pope of the church of one fails to realize that he does not even have power over himself; having closed himself off from the whole, his own perspective of the world restricts him. Rather, like St. Maximilian Kolbe, in giving ourselves to others, we find our true freedom by serving them as a way of serving Christ. Just as we are made for relationships in the natural order, so, too, are we made for relationships in the supernatural order.

The modern world, in rejecting the Church's vision of freedom and exalting its own mistaken version, acts like a child fighting his mother because he demands dessert without eating dinner. The fruits of the modern world—two world wars, a cold war, genocide on a mass scale, the eclipse of God from public life—should give us pause before accepting modernity's claims as true. We would do better, writes Romano Guardini, to trust the Church, which we call our holy mother for her tender care for us, with her 2,000-year perspective as a guide for how we ought to live.

> [O]f her very nature she thinks with the mind, not of any one race, but of the entire and Catholic world. She judges and lives, not by the insight of the passing moment, but by tradition. The latter, however, is the sum total of the collective experience of her past. She thus transcends local, national, and temporal limitations. . . . [S]he is not concerned with nations, but with humanity as a whole, and individual men and women.[5]

When we forsake the eternal teachings and perspectives of the Church for the limited fads of the modern world, we become enslaved to its demands, even as we think we

---

5. Guardini, *The Meaning of the Church*, 80–81.

are free. We find authentic freedom when we willingly entrust ourselves to the loving care and wisdom of our holy mother the Church, which desires nothing less than our eternal salvation.

The Church and the Sacraments

Our desire to be free from constraints points to another innate need that we feel: the need for salvation, for deliverance from that which threatens us.

Catholics believe unequivocally that salvation from our sins comes from Jesus Christ through his saving sacrifice on the Cross. God did not will our salvation through a nebulous, abstract, or imaginary manner. Knowing that we are corporeal beings with natural desires to see, touch, and feel, God became man so we could see and touch him. Then, in an incredible act of self-sacrifice, Christ allowed us to see our salvation as he felt it pierce his very flesh. When he rose triumphantly from the dead, manifesting his divinity and his victory over sin, he retained his physical body, which, though transformed, still bore the marks of the pain he endured.

If God willed to make his salvation visible and inclusive of the human body, it follows that he would also will the extension of his salvation in time to function in the same manner. As Fr. Colman O'Neill explains,

> Christ has given the Church more than his voice; he gives himself, his full humanity, his body which brought healing to the sick and the sinners of Palestine, and which, now that it is glorified in heaven, is the channel of being and life for his mystical body.[6]

O'Neill continues,

> The power of the risen Christ which will ultimately draw all the elect into the fullness of his resurrection is, as it were, filtered through the sacramental rite, producing in the recipient only a partial likeness to the glory of Christ.[7]

Sacraments can only do this because they flow from the Body of Christ.

We find a biblical model for this transferring of spiritual power via tangible means in the story of the woman seeking Jesus for relief from her hemorrhage (Mk 5:25–34): "If I touch even his garments I shall be made well." When Jesus asked who had touched him, his disciples were dismissive; with the crowds pressing in on him, it would be impossible to identify anyone. But Jesus knew that "power had gone forth from him" because she touched him with faith. "Daughter, your faith has made you well."

---

6. Colman O'Neill, *Meeting Christ in the Sacraments* (New York: Society of St. Paul/Alba House, 1991), 41.

7. Colman O'Neill, *Meeting Christ in the Sacraments*, 75–76.

The seven sacraments of the Church work in the same manner. We approach the sacraments in faith, knowing that through them we can be saved. But instead of reaching out to touch Christ, he reaches out to touch us through the signs of the sacraments.

The unique power that each of the sacraments has comes directly from Christ, who sends forth his grace through them, the figurative limbs of his body. Hence the sacraments flow from the Church to which Christ entrusted them. Christ's commands were clear: "Do this in memory of me." "Receive the Holy Spirit. If you forgive the sins of any, they are forgiven." "Go therefore and make disciples of all nations, baptizing them in the name of the Father and of the Son and of the Holy Spirit." "Heal the sick." "A man shall leave his father and mother and be joined to his wife, and the two shall become one. What therefore God has joined together, let no man put asunder." [8]

Christ's commands to spread his salvation through the sacraments come with another reminder: "Apart from me you can do nothing" (Jn 15:5). Only in the Church, joined with Christ the head, can we receive the sacraments. Because of Christ's direct connection to the Church, each of the sacraments transmits his

8. Lk 22:19; Jn 20:22–23; Mt 28:19; Mt 10:8; Mt 19:5–6.

salvation by means of the ritual words spoken by the Church's minister. The theological term for this miracle is "*ex opere operato*," meaning "from the work being performed." It is Christ, therefore, who performs the sacrament through bishops, priests, and deacons, who act as if they were electrical wires transferring power from its source to individual homes. The personal holiness of clergymen, or lack of it, has no bearing on the transmission of grace from Christ to his people.

The sacraments, therefore, have a twofold sense, as the *Catechism* explains.[9] They are "by the Church" insofar as they receive their efficacy from Christ as part of his body; and they are "for the Church" insofar as they exist to bring salvation to sinners, the members of Christ's body. Christ instituted each of the seven sacraments so that his supernatural grace could build upon the natural order while corresponding to the natural progression of human life.[10] From birth, to growth, to carrying out life's tasks, to death, the sacraments bring us God's grace to help us meet life's challenges so we can return back to God at the end of our earthly pilgrimages as his worthy servants.

As with Christ's Incarnation, all seven sacraments use human realities to communicate divine realities. Just

---

9. *CCC*, 1118.

10. *CCC*, 1210.

as it requires faith to see that Christ is God, it requires faith to see the divine realities transmitted through human means. The signs of the sacraments are efficacious, meaning each one actually does what it signifies.

Baptism is more than just a ritual initiation. Through baptism the infinitely generous Father incorporates us, his adopted sons and daughters, into his family to share his divine life with us. Our membership in Christ's body is permanent and irrevocable, regardless of the sins we commit, because baptism imparts a character, that is, a seal or a figurative mark, on the human soul together with sanctifying grace. We may lose the grace through sin (it can be restored through the sacrament of penance), but we can never lose the character. The character commissions us to worship God in this life and to live with him forever in the next. We can worship him because, baptized into Christ's body, we share also in Christ's priesthood, whereby he offered himself as the perfect sacrifice to God on behalf of all human beings.[11]

With baptism we also find the sign of water fulfilling a dual function that corresponds to its dual role as both a cleansing agent and as a source of life. In the supernatural order, in the words of St. Thomas Aquinas, baptism brings about "'regeneration,' which refers to

11. Aquinas, *Summa Theologiae*, III.63.2, III.63.3.

the fact that man begins the new life of righteousness; and 'enlightenment,' which refers especially to faith, by which man receives spiritual life."[12] The regeneration is a cleansing from both original sin, which is the deprivation of the original holiness that God intended for us at creation, and from any personal sins we have committed should we be baptized as teenagers or adults.

All human beings are born with original sin, passed on from Adam and Eve, by virtue of our common humanity, as St. Paul clearly teaches: "Sin came into the world through one man and death through sin. . . . [B]y one man's disobedience many were made sinners" (Rom 5:12, 19). This is why even infants must be baptized: as innocent as they may appear, they, too, possess a weakened human nature because of original sin and bear the burden of it.

The trials of life show us that to reach God in heaven we have to be more than prepared; we have to be fortified as we grow and meet new challenges. Like athletes who strengthen their muscles through constant exercise so that they can win their coveted championship, Catholics need their souls strengthened so they can live their vocation and overcome temptations to sin. For this we have the sacrament of confirmation.

---

12. Aquinas, *Summa Theologiae*, III.66.1.ad.1.

The very name of the sacrament explains its purpose: to confirm someone is to strengthen the individual, to validate his or her standing with an added assurance or aid. We cannot confirm ourselves: the act of confirmation is always directed outward, such as when we confirm events, commitments, or other people in a specific role. Our confirmation in Christ, therefore, can only come from the Church. The physical sign of the sacrament of confirmation is the anointing with oil, which, since the time of ancient Israel, symbolizes the consecration of someone for a particular task. By this anointing we are confirmed as Catholics to "share more completely in the mission of Jesus Christ and the fullness of the Holy Spirit with which he is filled."[13]

Confirmation, like baptism, imposes a permanent character on the soul that recalls ancient generals branding their soldiers with their personal seal. This is a helpful analogy, for through it we see both confirmation and the Church herself in a different light. First, in confirmation we are sealed as soldiers in Christ's army so that we can fight the forces of evil enticing us toward sin and succeed in our mission—which is Christ's mission—of bringing God's loving salvation to everyone.

Second, we can reflect on the members of Christ's body in their current states: those who now live with

13. *CCC*, 1294.

Christ in heaven are members of the Church triumphant, while those who are being purged of their sins in purgatory comprise the Church suffering. Those of us on earth, still struggling to reach our eternal destiny, form the Church militant.

Because of human weakness, we sometimes fail to do what God commands us, even as he offers us all the grace we need to carry out his orders. These failures are sins. In his mercy God has left us a means whereby we can be forgiven of our sins and return to his standard renewed. This means is the sacrament of reconciliation or penance in which we confess our sins to a priest to receive God's forgiveness.

So often we hear a singular objection about the sacrament of reconciliation: "Why do I have to confess my sins to a priest when I can confess them directly to God?" We confess our sins to a priest, who, in the confessional, functions as a channel of God's forgiveness, because we cannot make amends for our sins simply by thinking about them. Rather, we have to *do* something about them. Walking into the Church to seek God's forgiveness makes our confession real, removing it from the subjective realm. We should also not reject the command to go to confession on the grounds that the bishop or priest is just as much a sinner as we are. When we confess our sins, it is not the priest who forgives us, but

Christ who acts through him. Who the priest is or what he has done does not inhibit the merciful grace that God wants to give us.

There are two sacraments of vocation, or service, in the Church. One, holy orders, will be discussed in Chapter 4. The other, holy matrimony, may seem to be the furthest thing from holiness, especially with the prevalence of divorce and other marital difficulties today. Yet, if we consider the truly happy couples we have met, we see that it is possible to harness the grace of the sacrament to live a happy, and even holy, marriage. With God's grace, a couple's "mutual love becomes an image of the absolute and unfailing love with which God loves man."[14] Husband and wife are called to direct each other to God. They do so most effectively in the Church.

Amidst the cynicism that too often surrounds marriage, we can forget the countless examples of Christ-like sacrifice around us: the husband who takes a second job to support his family, the wife who stays awake with her sick child, the husband or wife who drops everything to be the caretaker of the other during those fraught final weeks and days of terminal illness. As part of Christ's body, we receive the fruits of his sacrifice so we can sacrifice for our spouse.

---

14. *CCC*, 1604.

Today we see an increasing number of Catholics foregoing marriage in the Church, and even foregoing marriage altogether in favor of "domestic partnerships" that plagiarize marriage's trappings but lack its vows of permanence and fidelity. Our culture's loss of faith certainly contributes to this phenomenon, but so, too, does a fear of the commitment that marriage requires. This is a double tragedy, for it is faith that gives us the courage to assume the commitment of marriage, and healthy marriages contribute to a healthy culture. By marrying in the Church, we receive the grace and the constant reminders we need to remember that the vocation of marriage is one of sacrifice for the other.

With sacramental aid at every stage of human life, it is fitting that there is also one for the seriously ill and dying: the anointing of the sick, which fortifies us spiritually to carry the cross of our illness and lightens the final steps of our journey home to God. In illness, especially terminal illness, we become completely dependent on other people to care for us and to provide for our basic needs. This is another reason why we receive this sacrament from the Church: we cannot persevere through our illness alone. In explaining the anointing of the sick, St. James teaches us the role of the Church in caring for the ill:

> Is any among you sick? Let him call for the elders of the church, and let them pray over him, anointing

> him with oil in the name of the Lord; and the prayer of faith will save the sick man, and the Lord will raise him up; and if he has committed sins, he will be forgiven. (Jas 5:14–15)

When possible, the anointing of the dying is followed by the reception of holy communion, known as *viaticum*, meaning "food for the way." At this moment, the Eucharist is the food needed for the final journey, the "sacrament of passing over from death to life, from this world to the Father."[15] There is no sacrament that brings us closer to God than the Eucharist. And there is no sacrament as essential to the Church as the Eucharist, upon which, in turn, the Church is completely dependent.

The Church and the Eucharist

The Eucharist is the sacrament *par excellence*. While the other six sacraments transmit Christ's grace, the Eucharist embodies grace as Christ himself, truly present among us under the appearance of bread and wine. The creator of the universe, having humbled himself once to become man, humbles himself still more as he transforms simple bread into his body.

At the last supper, when instituting the Eucharist, Jesus explained to the apostles how his impending death

---

15. *CCC*, 1525.

was his self-sacrifice for the world. Upon expiring, Jesus had his side pierced by a soldier with a lance, and immediately blood and water flowed out. With the blood and water—symbols of the Eucharist and baptism—Christ brought the Church into existence from his own heart.

To this day the Church's vitality comes from the Eucharist. Each time the Church celebrates the Mass anywhere in the world, Christ's once-and-for-all self-sacrifice on the Cross is re-presented before us. We are mystically transported to Calvary 2,000 years ago at the very moment when the world was redeemed. This is why the Mass is celebrated every single day, from east to west; it brings us back to the very reason and source of the Church's existence. As St. John Paul II summarizes, "the Eucharist builds the Church and the Church makes the Eucharist."[16]

To have the Mass and the Eucharist, we need the Church. Christ gave his command to "do this in memory of me" to the apostles alone. We can have a validly celebrated Mass because the priest, by virtue of his ordination, is brought into a chain of succession that links directly to the apostles, and, consequently, the last supper.[17] To have the Eucharist, we must have priests. To

16. John Paul II, Encyclical Letter on the Eucharist in its Relationship to the Church, *Ecclesia de Eucharistia* (April 17, 2003), 26. Vatican website: *www.vatican.va.*

17. John Paul II, *Ecclesia de Eucharistia*, 29.

have priests, we must have the Church, which is the only means whereby a man can be ordained into the unbroken chain of succession that extends to the apostles.

To protect this most precious gift, Christ entrusted the Eucharist to the apostles and their successors, the bishops, to preserve it through time and to protect it from harm. As St. John Paul writes, "the Eucharist is too great a gift to tolerate ambiguity and deception."[18] For this reason, the Church has established rules governing both the distribution and reception of Holy Communion. Among the latter kind, a person must be a baptized Catholic, not conscious of unconfessed mortal sin, not subject to ecclesiastical censure, and, excluding physical infirmity, fasting for one hour. The rules for reception have a twofold function. First, they protect the Eucharist from being profaned by those who are not properly prepared to receive this immense gift, just as we protect our valuables from damage by reserving them in secure locations. Second, they protect the would-be recipient from inflicting spiritual damage upon himself by receiving the Lord without adequate preparation. St. Paul is very direct on this topic: "Whoever, therefore, eats the bread or drinks the cup of the Lord in an unworthy manner will be guilty of profaning the body and blood of the Lord" (1 Cor 11: 27).

18. John Paul II, *Ecclesia de Eucharistia*, 10.

The Eucharist also brings us into communion with one another. "The Eucharist, precisely by building up the Church, creates human community."[19] Again, we turn to St. Paul:

> The cup of blessing which we bless, is it not a participation in the blood of Christ? The bread which we break, is it not a participation in the body of Christ? Because there is one bread, we who are many are one body, for we all partake of the one bread. (1 Cor 10:16–17)

Because of the infinite value of the Eucharist, this spiritual communion with our fellow Catholics has to be supported by a prior, visible communion with the Church's structures that guarantee the Eucharist and the Faith. This includes communion, in the sense of willing obedience, with the pope and the bishops who govern the Church; acceptance of the Church's dogmatic teachings on faith and morals; and participation in the sacraments by attending Mass each Sunday. If any of the exterior forms of communion are lacking to any degree (such as is the case with non-Catholics, with apostates who have willfully rejected the Faith, and with unrepentant sinners) the invisible communion with Christ and with other Catholics will inevitably grow shallow and stale.

---

19. John Paul II, *Ecclesia de Eucharistia*, 24.

The Eucharist teaches us that the Church does not exist simply to perform sacraments, but that she herself is a sacramental mystery that does what she is. She, as his body, makes visible to the world Jesus Christ, in whom "we live and move and have our being" (Acts 17:28). She is the means through which Christ fulfills his own promise to be with us to the close of the age. The Church, therefore, could not have been some post-resurrection invention or afterthought. No, God destined the Church before he created the world.

3

Did Jesus found a Church?

Jesus made noticeably few statements about the Church in the Gospels. Should not Jesus have been more explicit, it is argued, if he really had wanted an institution to succeed him? Upon closer examination we see that not only did Jesus intend for the Church to carry on his mission, but during his ministry he also laid down all her groundwork.

Before looking at the Church's founding, it is important to consider Jesus' method of instruction. In certain cases, Jesus' commands need no interpretation: "Love one another, even as I have loved you" (Jn 13:34). "Pray then like this" (Mt 6:9). "When you fast, anoint your head and wash your face, that your fasting may not be seen by men but by your Father" (Mt 6:17–18).

Yet in so many other instances, rather than hand us a blueprint to follow, Jesus taught with parables, stories with thought-provoking meanings that often require interpretation. And he did not apologize for his occasionally perplexing method:

> To you [the twelve apostles] has been given the secret to the kingdom of God, but for those outside everything is in parables; so that they may indeed see but not perceive, and may indeed hear but not understand; lest they should turn again, and be forgiven. (Mk 4:11–12)

Rather than give us the easy answer, Jesus willed for us to make the connections ourselves with the help of the Holy Spirit:

> It is your advantage that I go away, for if I do not go away, the Counselor will not come to you; but if I go, I will send him to you. . . . When the Spirit of truth comes, he will guide you into all the truth; for he will not speak on his own authority, but whatever he hears he will speak, *and he will declare to you the things that are to come.** (Jn 16:7, 13)

When the Holy Spirit burst forth on Pentecost, the apostles finally understood that, throughout his ministry, Christ was preparing the foundation for his Church to perpetuate his salvation until the end of time. As with Christ, the Church cannot be understood as a

---

* Emphasis added.

brand-new event, but as the culmination of all salvation history as recorded in the Old Testament. From the beginning of creation, God gradually prepared the world for the Church's foundation, just as he prepared the world for the Son's birth. The Incarnation is incomprehensible without the Old Testament. The same is true for the Church, the Incarnation's temporal extension.

When God initiated his covenant with Abraham, he established a lasting, personal relationship not just with one individual, but with an entire people whom he wished to call his own:

> I will establish my covenant between me and you and your descendants after you throughout the generations for an everlasting covenant, to be God to you and to your descendants after you. (Gen 17:7)

This covenant exacted a physical cost: the loss of skin and the shedding of blood in circumcision. By it, God showed that his love for us, and ours for him, is deeply intimate, reaching to the level of life itself. It also showed what God was asking of his people, as St. Cyril of Alexandria explains:

> "True circumcision is the perfect observance of the law, the cutting away and removing of everything alien to God and the ability to pass beyond worldly

things to approach the transcendent realities through understanding."[1]

Centuries later with the Mosaic covenant, the people of God received a mission here on earth. Constituted now as a nation among others, Israel is to be holy, set aside for God and serving as a priestly people that would point other nations to God. The sign of this covenant was the Ten Commandments, which, as the *Catechism* explains, open "a path to life . . . freed from the slavery of sin."[2] Like circumcision, this new covenant had a physical dimension: the Ten Commandments were written on stone tablets and retained in a gilded box, or ark. God's promise to Israel as he gave the commandments is clear:

> If you obey the commandments . . . by loving the Lord your God, by walking in his ways, and by keeping his commandments and his statutes and his ordinances, then you shall live and multiply, and the Lord your God will bless you." (Deut 30:16)[3]

---

1. Cyril of Alexandria, "Catena on Genesis, 3.1026" in *Ancient Christian Commentary on Scripture: Genesis 12–50*, ed. Mark Sheridan (Downers Grove, Illinois: InterVarsity Press, 2002), 54.

2. *CCC*, 2057.

3. Quoted in *CCC*, 2057.

In this final covenant of the Old Testament, God does not ask for obedience in return as he did with Abraham and Moses. He offers instead an unconditional covenant with David that would be realized in the most unsuspected of ways: through the Incarnation of the Son of God.[4]

We see in the three Old Testament covenants with Abraham, Moses, and David all the essential elements of the Church. The Church is the people of God, called out from the world to enter into a lasting relationship with him. God offers this people the new law of love to inaugurate a new way of living. He also provides physical signs of his covenant in the sacraments, with baptism taking the place of circumcision as the rite of initiation. God constituted the Church as the "light of the world" for those peoples and nations who do not believe so that "they may see your good works and give glory to your Father who is in heaven" (Mt 5:14, 16).

The great difference between the Church of the new covenant and the people of God of the old covenant is membership: the latter were born in the flesh, so this people was limited to a single nation, Israel. The new covenant, by contrast, is universal, for Christ "died for

---

4. *Introduction to Catholicism*, 2nd ed., ed. by Jeffrey Cole (Downers Grove, Illinois: Midwest Theological Forum, 2018), 96–97.

all, that those who live might live no longer for themselves but for him who for their sake died and was raised" (2 Cor 5:15).

Jesus made clear that he was not founding his own distinct community,[5] but was creating a new Israel for a universal mission through the commissioning of the twelve apostles, the new covenantal heirs of the twelve tribes of Israel. Jesus called the twelve apostles deliberately from among his disciples, after he had spent a whole night in prayer. That the Gospel writers named all twelve shows their immense importance to the Church. They were appointed "to be with him, and to be sent out to preach and have authority to cast out demons" (Mk 3:14–15). Since "apostle" means "one who is sent," the apostles take the role of the twelve tribes to a new level: they are not just the leaders of God's people, but they also must increase the ranks of his people.

As mentioned, Jesus chose Simon to be their leader. Like Abraham before him, Simon's new name signifies his new mission and the special relationship he has with God as the "rock," the human foundation for his Church:

---

5. International Theological Commission, *Select Themes of Ecclesiology on the Occasion of the Twentieth Anniversary of the Closing of the Second Vatican Council* (1984), I.3. Vatican website: *www.vatican.va.*

> And I tell you, you are Peter, and on this rock I will build my Church, and the gates of Hades shall not prevail against it. I will give you the keys of the kingdom of heaven, and whatever you bind on earth shall be bound in heaven, and whatever you loose on earth shall be loosed in heaven. (Mt 16:18–19)

It is one statement, but it is emphatic: Jesus intended to found a Church, a community of believers united to him with a leader at the helm. Just as the apostles' mission stems directly from the twelve tribes of Israel, Peter's specific vocation as the rock of the Church, holding the keys to the kingdom of heaven, has antecedents in the old covenant, when God entrusted Eliakim with authority over the temple in Jerusalem:

> And I will place on his shoulder the key of the house of David; he shall open, and none shall shut; and he shall shut, and none shall open. And I will fasten him like a peg in a sure place, and he will become a throne of honor to his father's house. (Is 22:22–23)

The authority of Peter is broader than that of Eliakim, who received custody of the physical temple. Christ gives Peter custody of the entire Church, with the task of serving as his vicar here on earth. The keys are the symbol of ruling authority, and the powers to bind and loose mean that Peter can make people subject to or freed from certain laws. That he can do so on earth as it is in heaven shows that his authority touches both the Church militant here on earth as well as the Church suffering and Church triumphant in eternity.

The antecedents in the Old Testament and the commissioning of the twelve apostles are not the only signs of Jesus' intention to found a Church. At the Last Supper he twice mentioned a desire for unity among his disciples. First, he instructed the apostles directly:

> Abide in me, and I in you. As the branch cannot bear fruit by itself, unless it abides in the vine, neither can you, unless you abide in me. I am the vine, you are the branches. He who abides in me, and I in him, he it is that bears much fruit. (Jn 15:4–5)

This analogy complements that of the Church as the Body of Christ, for here Jesus speaks of the profound connection between himself and his disciples; the vine is the life-giving source of the branches, just as he is the life-giving source of his members.

Further, in his final prayer to the Father before departing for the garden of Gethsemane, Jesus prayed earnestly for the disciples "whom thou hast given me" that his Father "keep them in thy name . . . that they may be one, even as we are one" (Jn 17:9, 11). He continued,

> I do not pray for these only, but also for those who believe in me through their word, that they may all be one; even as thou, Father, art in me, and I in thee, that they also may be in us, so that the world may believe that thou hast sent me. (Jn 17:20–21)

In extending his petition beyond his current disciples to those of the future, Jesus prayed for the unity of his people.

The Old Testament antecedents, combined with Christ's actions and prayers, unquestionably point the way toward his will to establish an institution to succeed him. But because the mystery of Christ himself could not be understood until after his death, resurrection, and ascension, the same is true of the Church. In fact, by Jesus' own reckoning, the Church had to look different during his earthly ministry than it would after his ascension:

> Can the wedding guests fast while the bridegroom is with them? As long as they have the bridegroom with them, they cannot fast. The days will come, when the bridegroom is taken away from them, and then they will fast on that day. (Mk 2:19–20)

When the bridegroom was taken away, two events completed the apostles' formation. The first was Jesus' death on the cross, the significance of which he interpreted for his apostles hours earlier in instituting the Eucharist. The cross serves as Christ's unlikely throne as the head of the Church, from whence he gives life to all his members through the blood and water poured out from his pierced side.[6]

The second was Pentecost, the final act in establishing the Church. In the summary of Pius XII,

> the Divine Redeemer began the building of the mystical temple of the Church when by his preaching he made known his precepts; he completed it when he hung glorified on the Cross; and he manifested and proclaimed it when he sent the Holy Spirit as Paraclete in visible form on his disciples.[7]

Pentecost fulfilled the promise Christ made to his disciples just before he ascended into heaven: "You shall receive power when the Holy Spirit has come upon you; and you shall be my witnesses in Jerusalem and in all Judea and Samaria and to the end of the earth" (Acts 1:8).

The divine power they received finally helped them to understand the mystery of Christ, which they had still not completely comprehended at his ascension nine

---

6. Pius XII, *Mystici Corporis Christi*, 30.

7. Pius XII, *Mystici Corporis Christi*, 26.

days earlier, and to preach his salvation without fear. On that first Pentecost the apostles "began to speak in other tongues, as the Spirit gave them utterance" (Acts 2:4). Peter then preached the first homily, explaining who Jesus of Nazareth was in light of Old Testament prophecy: "Let all the house of Israel therefore know assuredly that God has made him both Lord and Christ, this Jesus whom you crucified" (Acts 2:36). Having proclaimed Christ as the infant Church's focus, Peter then instructed the crowd how the Church would lead people to him: "Repent, and be baptized every one of you in the name of Jesus Christ for the forgiveness of sins; and you shall receive the gift of the Holy Spirit" (Acts 2:38).

Pentecost is called the birthday of the Church, and for good reason. What was hidden from the world as a seed suddenly burst forth, having been watered from Christ's own side and tilled by the Holy Spirit, as a fully-grown flower for the whole world to see as she began to carry out her divinely-constituted mission.

The Kingdom of God and the Church

The phrase "kingdom of God" is mentioned 122 times in the New Testament, 90 times from the lips of Jesus.[8]

8. Benedict XVI, *Jesus of Nazareth: From the Baptism in the Jordan to the Transfiguration*, trans. Adrian J. Walker (New York: Doubleday, 2007), 47.

Clearly the kingdom of God is a priority of Jesus' message, yet he never gives it a straight definition. The ambiguity has prompted one observer to quip that Jesus preached the kingdom of God, and what followed was the Church.[9] Benedict XVI comments that both irony and sadness can be detected in this observation:

> Instead of the great expectation of God's own Kingdom, of a new world transformed by God himself, we got something quite different—and what a pathetic substitute it is: the Church.[10]

Implicit in this criticism is not just the failure of Church members to live up to what they profess. It is the question of whether the Church got her message wrong from the very beginning. Should she have been preaching not about Jesus and his Cross, but about the kingdom of God—as Jesus did—as a community of peace and love?

In the modern era, explains Benedict XVI, biblical interpreters have emphasized Jesus' statements about the kingdom that associate its proclamation with the end of time, when God will begin his definitive reign over the

---

9. Benedict XVI, *Jesus of Nazareth*, 48. See Alfred Loisy, *L'Évangile et L'Église*.

10. Benedict XVI, *Jesus of Nazareth*, 48.

earth.[11] Each time we pray the Our Father, for example, we pray "thy kingdom come," pointing to an undetermined moment in the future. The same goes for the Beatitudes, which promise that the kingdom of God belongs to the poor in spirit and the persecuted. More recently, interpreters who view God and the Church as divisive have crafted a completely secular reading of "the kingdom" as "simply the name for a world governed by peace, justice, and the conservation of creation. . . . The 'Kingdom' is said to be the goal of history that has to be attained."[12]

It is impossible to justify these views if we consider all that Jesus said about the kingdom. It is the kingdom *of God*, or, synonymously, the kingdom *of heaven*, first and foremost, and not the kingdom of human beings. Second, even as the kingdom of God still awaits fulfillment in the future, there is an aspect of the kingdom immediately present in the person of Jesus. "If it is by the spirit of God that I cast out demons, then the kingdom of God has come upon you" (Mt 12:28).

By insisting that the kingdom of God is at hand, Jesus reveals that he, the Son of God, is the manifestation and the personification of the kingdom. God's kingdom is now present because Christ is present,

---

11. Benedict XVI, *Jesus of Nazareth*, 52.

12. Benedict XVI, *Jesus of Nazareth*, 53–54.

with the final consummation of the kingdom awaiting his second coming at the end of time. In Benedict's summary of Jesus' preaching on this topic,

> God is always at the center of the discussion, yet because Jesus himself is God—the Son—his entire preaching is a message about the mystery of his person, it is a Christology, that is, a discourse concerning God's presence in his own action and being.[13]

In other words, in proclaiming the kingdom, Jesus was proclaiming himself as God among us.

The Church, then, was right to center her message on the person of Christ from the very beginning, just as Peter did on the first Pentecost. The Church is not the manifestation of the kingdom of God as if she were an earthly utopia. Rather, in preaching Christ, the Church announces the kingdom that promises an infinitely loving communion with the holy Trinity, one that begins with baptism and is consummated after our death.

The Universal Church and the Local Church

When we are baptized, we are typically brought to our local parish, where the priest prays the words of

13. Benedict XVI, *Jesus of Nazareth*, 63.

the Lord as he pours the water onto the head of the candidate: "I baptize you in the name of the Father, and of the Son, and of the Holy Spirit." Regardless of what parish church we are baptized in, be it in New York or New Delhi, there is still one, single, universal Catholic Church, of which each parish across the world is an expression. As St. Paul teaches, "You were called to the one hope that belongs to your call, one Lord, one faith, one baptism, one God and Father of us all" (Eph 4:4–6). So, wherever we are baptized, we are incorporated instantly into the one universal Catholic Church.

This Church that flowered on Pentecost has spread throughout the world and is exhibited in every Catholic diocese, parish church, shrine, and retreat house. To be in any one of these particular places is to be in the one Universal Church. The Universal Church is not the sum of all the local churches, nor is she a federation of united local churches.[14] It is the task of the pope, the bishop of Rome and the successor of St. Peter, to guard the unity of the Church. In the words of the Second Vatican Council,

---

14. Congregation for the Doctrine of the Faith, *Letter to the Bishops of the Catholic Church on Some Aspects of the Church Understood as Communion* (May 28, 1992), 9. Vatican website: *www.vatican.va.*

> within the Church particular churches [i.e., dioceses] hold a rightful place; these Churches retain their own traditions, without in any way opposing the primacy of the Chair of Peter, which presides over the whole assembly of charity and protects legitimate differences, while at the same time assuring that such differences do not hinder unity but rather contribute toward it.[15]

The Universal Church is administrated on the local level through geographical territories called dioceses. Each diocese is, and must be, governed by a bishop, who, as a successor of the apostles, is the bridge that connects the individual diocese directly to all other dioceses and to the Universal Church. This is why at every Mass we pray for the Church "together with your servant (name) our pope and (name) our bishop." Through the pope and the bishops, we trace our faith directly to Christ and the twelve apostles.

As head of the Church, the Lord guarantees the integrity of our faith and baptism. This is a critical point, because, we, the human members of the Church, too often obscure our unity and the lofty gifts the Church offers us in every parish in the world. There can be problems with the pastor of the parish: a brusque personality, a

15. *Lumen Gentium,* 13.

disinterested approach, a seeming obsession with money or other non-spiritual things; there can be problems with the programs offered by the parish: poorly organized, not meeting the needs of the people, directors who are self-righteous or just plain annoying; and there can be problems with the people in the parish who often quarrel, just as with the people in the primitive church of Corinth that St. Paul was addressing. Personal shortcomings mitigate the Church's effectiveness in the world, but they do not undermine her mission or her divine elements. If anything, they confirm the need for the Church as an instrument of grace among sinners. Our goal as followers of Christ is not perfection, but conversion, the constant moving of the sincere, humble heart to God.

If we do not allow utopian fantasies of human perfection to cloud our vision, we can see that the local church, with all its limitations, puts us in communion with the Universal Church and with Christ himself, not because of the leaders and people within them, but because of what God has given the Church. Among these gifts is her hierarchy, to whose nature and purpose we now turn.

4

Why priests and bishops?

The Catholic Church has both a supernatural and a natural leadership structure. She has a divine head, and so is ultimately ruled by Jesus Christ. As an association of human beings on earth, the Church is also ruled by men who, with Christ's authority, aid their fellow Catholics in fulfilling God's will. These men constitute the Church's hierarchy—the pope, bishops, and priests who govern the Church militant here on earth.

We have already seen the essential role that the apostles played in the Church and the necessity of our living connection with them. We have also seen that Christ intentionally established the Church and designated Peter to be her visible foundation. It remains to look at the Church's governing structure in more detail, as it is essential to her life and to understanding her perennial challenges.

Apostle, as mentioned in Chapter 3, means one who is sent, and Jesus sent the twelve apostles to carry out his mission of teaching. After giving Peter alone the keys to the kingdom and the power to bind and loose, Jesus then gave the twelve, united as a single college, the power to bind and loose (Mt 18:18). In addition to teaching and governing authority, Jesus also gave the apostles one other gift that can be easily overlooked: he made them priests. Benedict XVI points out that in Mark's Gospel, the calling of the twelve intentionally echoes the Old Testament terminology for appointment to the priesthood. "Mark thus presents the apostolic ministry as a fusion of the priestly and prophetic missions."[1] This fusion was completed at the Last Supper. When Jesus instituted the Eucharist, he also instituted the priesthood of the new covenant as he commissioned the twelve to "do this in memory of me," which "put a eucharistic seal on their mission."[2] Finally, after he rose from the dead, Jesus also gave his new priests the power to forgive sins: "He breathed on them, and said to them,

---

1. Benedict XVI, *Jesus of Nazareth*, 171.

2. John Paul II, *Letter to Priests for Holy Thursday 2004* (April 6, 2004), 3. Vatican website: *www.vatican.va.*

'Receive the Holy Spirit. If you forgive the sins of any, they are forgiven; if you retain the sins of any, they are retained'" (Jn 20:22–23).

Hence the apostles received a threefold mission at Pentecost: they were to teach, to sanctify, and to govern, and none of these functions could be separated from the others. Appointed to teach and to bind, they were also ordained as priests to offer the sacrifice of Christ on behalf of the people. The office of apostle, then, is one of service to the faithful.

Since a principle of leadership existed in Israel and in the first days of the Church, it stands to reason that Christ intended that the authority he entrusted to his apostles be passed on to their successors. St. Paul urges Timothy, a bishop, not to "neglect the gift you have, which was given you by the prophetic utterance when the elders laid their hands upon you" (1 Tim 4:13–14). Likewise, when the apostles chose the first seven deacons to serve the Church in Jerusalem, the apostles "prayed and laid their hands upon them" (Acts 6:6).

St. Irenaeus of Lyons (130–202), after naming, to his own time, the twelve men who had succeeded St. Peter as the bishops of Rome, declares that

> by this succession, the ecclesiastical tradition from the apostles, and the preaching of the truth, have come down to us. And this is most abundant proof that

> there is one and the same vivifying faith, which has been preserved in the Church from the apostles to the present.[3]

The sacrament of holy orders, like baptism and confirmation, imparts a permanent character that forever alters men to serve God by configuring them to Christ the high priest. There are three degrees of holy orders, each with its own indelible character and its own degree of sacred power. The highest degree is that of bishop, when men are ordained into the apostolic mission of teaching, sanctifying, and governing. Because of the enormity of this task, bishops delegate a circumscribed element of their authority to men whom they ordain as priests, called *presbyteroi* in the New Testament, to aid them in fulfilling their office. Priests offer the sacraments, teach, govern their parishes, and perform other responsibilities, always and only with the authorization of the bishop in whose territory they reside. The lowest level of holy orders is conferred upon deacons, or servants, who are delegated a limited authority to facilitate the ministry of the bishop and priest.

Having been configured to the Son of Man and having received power to act in his person, bishops, priests,

---

3. Irenaeus of Lyons, *Adversus Haereses*, III, 3, in *Ante-Nicene Fathers*, Vol. 1 (New York: Charles Scribner's Sons, 1903), 416.

and deacons are ordained to a life of service within the Church. They are to teach the faithful the ways of God; they direct them toward holiness and away from sin; they sanctify them through the sacraments, prayer, and fellowship. In practical terms, their lives revolve around ensuring the religious education of all the faithful, administering the sacraments, and providing opportunities for the faithful to grow in faith, hope, and charity. Celebrating the Mass encompasses the very heart of episcopal and priestly ministry, for through it they continue, and share more deeply in, Christ's own priesthood here on earth.

As successors of the apostles, bishops "take the place of Christ himself, teacher, shepherd, and priest, and act as his representatives" within their respective dioceses.[4] Bishops are directly responsible for the entirety of Catholic life within their dioceses, from the celebration of the sacraments; to the establishment or closure of parishes and schools; to the workings of priests, deacons, seminarians, and lay personnel employed by the diocese; to Church-sponsored charitable activities; to the physical property owned by the diocese. In these countless manifestations of the Church's universal mission, each bishop is called

4. *Lumen Gentium*, 21.

to serve as the spiritual father of his people. Bishops exercise their authority in union with the pope, who, as vicar of Christ on earth, exercises jurisdiction over the Universal Church. The Second Vatican Council clearly teaches that the college of bishops has

> no authority unless united with the Roman Pontiff, Peter's successor, as its head . . . For the Roman Pontiff, by reason of his office as Vicar of Christ, namely, and as pastor of the entire Church, has full, supreme, and universal power over the whole Church.[5]

It is one thing to read the Church's constitution and the beautiful vocation of the hierarchy. It is quite another to read it knowing that bishops often fall short of their call. It is fair to ask: Why ought we obey bishops and support them with our financial contributions? It may be tempting in the midst of scandal to leave the Church and follow Jesus on our own.

It is as if Jesus was preparing us for facing this very conundrum in hammering the Pharisees, the Jewish religious leaders of his day, for their hypocrisy in binding the common people with heavy religious obligations while exempting themselves. Jesus excoriates them as

---

5. *Lumen Gentium*, 22.

a "brood of vipers," "blind guides," and "whitewashed tombs, which outwardly appear beautiful, but within they are filled with dead men's bones and all uncleanness" (Mt 23:16, 27, 33).

Nevertheless, Jesus instructed his fellow Jews to obey them: "The scribes and the Pharisees sit on Moses' seat; so practice and observe whatever they tell you" (Mt 23:2–3).

We can see Jesus giving the same instruction to us today. We are to obey the bishops because of their office, not because of who they are as individuals or how they behave. Jesus is clear: do what they say, not what they do. For what they say—the teachings we are to believe and the moral life we are to lead—is not their own personal teaching, but what Christ says.

Just as the grace of the sacraments transcends the person of the bishop, so, too, does the deposit of faith, the substance of all our beliefs and practices as Catholics, transcend his person. The deposit of faith that has been entrusted to the Church belongs, ultimately, not to men, but to Christ, who promised that "heaven and earth will pass away, but my words will not pass away" (Mt 24:35). Individual bishops will pass away and will receive their eternal reward—or punishment—as God sees fit. Yet bishops, united as a college with the pope ensuring their unity, remain essential to our Faith because their direct connection to the apostles ensures that everything that Christ deposited with them does not pass away, but reaches us in its fullness.

We will look at the bishops' specific teaching authority in more detail in the next chapter. For now it remains to consider how the faithful ought to respond to bishops as they exercise their legitimate governing authority. First, we should remember that most bishops are striving for holiness, just like most of their people. There are numberless saints among them, some canonized and many more that are lost to history, known only to God and the people they governed. We can count Sts. Patrick, Augustine, Ambrose, John Chrysostom, Thomas Beckett, Francis de Sales, and John Neumann as just a few saints among the bishops, while of the popes, eighty-three of the 266 who have sat on the chair of Peter have been saints and martyrs.

Second, regardless of the personal holiness of the bishop, we must recognize that he possesses legitimate authority by the power of his ordination. As members of the Church, we are subject to the bishop's jurisdiction as set forth by the Church's own laws, just as, in the professional world, we are subject to the authority of a company or organization's rules.

Third, we should *want* to heed our bishops. The Second Vatican Council exhorts that the faithful

> should be closely attached to the bishop as the Church is to Jesus Christ, and as Jesus Christ is to the Father, so that all things may conspire towards harmonious unity, and bring forth abundant fruit unto the glory of God.[6]

We should support our bishops continually by our prayers, and we ought to encourage them whenever possible through personal greetings, letters, or through intermediaries such as our pastors. When we are united with our bishops in prayer, charity, and good will, the Church is stronger, we feel stronger in our own faith, and our collective witness to the world is more attractive.

Fourth, when a bishop makes a decision that we think is not beneficial for the people, we are in our right to contact him and to ask him to reconsider.

Church history gives us an example to follow, that of St. Catherine of Siena, who implored Pope Gregory XI to leave his palace at Avignon, France, and return to his rightful diocese in Rome. St. Catherine wrote the pope several letters and made the arduous journey to visit him in 1375. She wrote with charity, yet she did not mince words: "I beg of you, on behalf of Christ crucified, that you be not a timorous child, but manly. Open your

---

6. *Lumen Gentium*, 27.

mouth, and swallow down the bitter for the sweet."[7] The saint continued,

> Answer God, who calls you to hold and possess the seat of the glorious Shepherd St. Peter, whose vicar you have been. And raise the standard of the holy Cross. . . . In this way you will come and attain the reformation, giving good priests to holy Church. . . . [C]ome, father, and no longer make to wait the servants of God, who afflict themselves in desire.[8]

Finally, in 1377, despite voices urging the waffling pontiff to remain in France, Gregory returned to Rome. St. Catherine's entreaties were successful but required two years of prayerful perseverance for reform to occur. It is worth noting that another heroic saint, Bridget of Sweden, also worked valiantly to bring the pope back to Rome, but she died in 1373, never to see the fruit of her labor.

From St. Catherine and St. Bridget, we learn that the faithful can intervene with the hierarchy, but only with prayer, perseverance, and personal holiness. It was this last quality, above all, that converted Pope Gregory. Evil

---

7. St. Catherine of Siena, *St. Catherine of Siena as Seen in her Letters*, trans. and ed. Vida D. Scudder (New York: E.P. Dutton & Co., 1905), 185.

8. St. Catherine of Siena, *St. Catherine of Siena as Seen in her Letters*, 132–133.

cannot be cast out by evil, but only by good. We also have to be willing to suffer for the Church's purification, just as Christ did on the Cross and these saints did in scaling mountains on their journeys. And we may not see a resolution in our own lifetimes; we must trust, as St. Bridget did, that renewal will come in God's time, even if we find that wait dissatisfying on a personal level.

Two tactics recently wielded by the faithful to combat corruption are staying home from Mass and withholding donations. The former can never be an option. If we skip Mass willfully as a statement of protest, we cut off our noses to spite our faces, for we are cutting ourselves off from Christ. Not only do we hurt ourselves by depriving ourselves of divine grace, we do nothing at all to solve the problem. At Mass we can at least pray for a solution; at home, alone and angry, we can accomplish nothing to benefit the Church. In fact, staying home in protest can have a seriously negative effect on us: it feeds our egos and turns us into Pharisees as we set ourselves up as arbiters of righteousness.

Withholding donations to the Church can be an effective means for the faithful to express their displeasure to their bishops, but it has to be done in two ways. First, a person must discern carefully through prayer whether this is the right step to take. As Catholics we are obliged to support the material needs of the Church. We may not realize that our donations to, say, the bishop's annual appeal or to a diocesan collection, go to some very needy places and important causes: food for the poor, shelters for unwed mothers, Catholic grammar school tuition aid, training of future priests, maintenance to diocesan shrines or other properties. Cutting off funds to the bishop will hurt the worthy causes that depend on these donations. Second, should a person decide to withhold money, he must inform the bishop by letter of his decision; otherwise, his protest remains unknown.

Reform is always the goal of the human dimension of the Church because sin and weakness are always a part of human life. St. Catherine of Siena wisely realized what Pope Gregory XI seemed to have forgotten: that the Church has flourished

> when men took note of nothing but the honor of God and the salvation of souls, caring for spiritual things and not temporal. For ever since [the Church] has aimed more at temporal than at spiritual, things have gone from bad to worse.[9]

Every crisis in the Church, including our current one, is caused by the same error: Church members who seek the temporal more eagerly than the spiritual.

---

9. St. Catherine of Siena, *St. Catherine of Siena as Seen in her Letters*, 131.

The Priesthood: Challenges and Aspirations

One prominent sign of priestly service is the observance of perpetual, celibate chastity, a discipline that has been the subject of great controversy. Like the covenants and the sacraments, celibacy is a physical sign of a deeper spiritual reality: the love of Christ for his bride, the Church, which is emulated by bishops and priests who, out of love for the Church, give themselves completely to the people they are called to serve. St. John Paul explains the reason why a priest does not take a wife or have a family: "The heart of the priest, in order that it may be available for this service, must be free. Celibacy is a sign of a freedom that exists for the sake of service."[10] Celibacy makes the priest free for the benefit of all the people of God. and out of touch with intimacy. compassum

By abstaining from marriage, bishops and priests imitate the practice of Christ to whom they have been configured by ordination. The Second Vatican Council calls celibacy "a precious gift" to the Church because by it clergy

> adhere to [Christ] more easily with an undivided
> heart, they dedicate themselves more freely in him

10. John Paul II, *Letter to all the Priests on the Occasion of Holy Thursday 1979* (April 8, 1979), 8. Vatican website: *www.vatican.va.*

> and through him to the service of God and men, and they more expeditiously minister to his Kingdom and the work of heavenly regeneration. . . . They give, moreover, a living sign of the world to come, by a faith and charity already made present, in which the children of the resurrection neither marry nor take wives.[11]

The celibate priest, who becomes free to serve others by dying to himself and to his natural desires, reminds us that it is not the natural world, but the supernatural world that is our true home.

Celibacy has been blamed for the diminishing number of vocations to the priesthood in recent years. In calling some to celibacy "for the sake of the kingdom of heaven," Jesus includes this proviso: "He who is able to receive this, let him receive it" (Mt 19:12). Celibacy, and therefore, the priesthood, are not for everyone. But they are for some, and those willing to respond to God's call to be configured to his Son

> should all the more humbly and steadfastly pray with the Church for that grace of fidelity, which is never denied to those who seek it, and use all the

11. Decree on the Ministry and Life of Priests, *Presbyterorum Ordinis* (December 7, 1965), 16. Vatican website: *www.vatican.va*.

supernatural and natural aids available to remain faithful to their promise.[12]

If we consider the ideal priest, an essential quality is the ability to put aside his own desires for the sake of his people. The willingness and the ability to maintain the discipline of celibate chastity is a significant step in that direction. It does not guarantee perfection nor the power to die to self in every situation, but it does show that the priest is willing to give all he has to God for the good of the Church. That man is the priest we want. In the words of St. John Paul, "The Church, as the spouse of Jesus Christ, wishes to be loved by the priest in the total and exclusive manner in which Jesus Christ her head and spouse loved her."[13]

No, celibacy is not the cause of a decline in men willing to become priests. The discipline has existed for many centuries; the decline in priests is only a phenomenon of recent decades. The decline is a result of a crisis of faith—of a lack of faith in God, in Christ, and in the Church. Why would a man want to be conformed to Christ whom he does not love? Why would a man give his life to serve

---

12. *Presbyterorum Ordinis*, 16.

13. John Paul II, Post-Synodal Apostolic Exhortation on the Formation of Priests in the Circumstances of the Present Day, *Pastores Dabo Vobis* (March 15, 1992), 29. Vatican website: *www.vatican.va.*

a Church that he does not fully appreciate? The number and the quality of priests we have is indicative of the spiritual health of the Body of Christ that hands on the Faith to potential priests. When we, the members of the body, love Christ as we ought, we will find more men willing to answer the call to serve as priests.

Nor is celibacy the cause of the sexual abuse of children that has been perpetrated by hundreds of priests across the country, particularly in the 1960s, 1970s, and 1980s. Blaming celibacy is symptomatic of the lie imbibed from the sexual revolution, namely, that the sexual impulse is destined to be indulged. As Fr. Carter Griffin writes, "sexual abuse is no more caused by being celibate than adultery is caused by being married."[14] In other words, marital infidelity is caused by a failure to maintain one's marriage vow, not by marriage itself. Likewise, sexual failures by priests are caused by their failure to live up to their vocation, not by celibacy itself.

What did cause the widespread outbreak of sexual abuse? It is common to consider a number of social factors, and there are several: the failure to present with conviction the Church's teachings on human sexuality in seminaries and schools; the dangerous influences of

---

14. Carter Griffin, *Why Celibacy? Reclaiming the Fatherhood of the Priest* (Steubenville, Ohio: Emmaus Road Publishing, 2019), 90.

the sexual revolution and an increasingly libertine culture; and the ordination of psychologically immature men to the priesthood.[15] Beneath all these social factors is a deeper flaw, the same mentioned by St. Catherine of Siena in combating another form of corruption among the clergy: allowing a desire for the temporal to eclipse the love of God. Benedict XVI puts the matter directly: "Only where faith no longer determines the actions of man are such offenses possible."[16] Priests are ordained to bring us the invisible gifts of God. When the physical and the temporal become our end instead of our means to God, we sin—we choose ourselves over God. The current crisis of the Church has resulted from, at bottom, thousands of individual sins by priests and bishops who put their base, personal desires ahead of God and his people.

Another perpetual source of confusion about the priesthood is its reservation to men only. As equality between the sexes has become a major focus of our society, it remains noteworthy that the Church's most prominent role, the priest who offers Mass for the people, is

---

15. See Benedict XVI, "The Church and the scandal of sexual abuse," *Catholic News Agency*, April 10, 2019, and Sullins, "Is Catholic clergy sex abuse related to homosexual priests?" (Lake Charles, Louisiana: The Ruth Institute, 2018).

16. Benedict XVI, "The Church and the scandal of sexual abuse."

not available to women. The Church's rules on this are little understood and perceived as antiquated at best, downright sexist at worst.

One major difficulty in understanding the Church's teaching is that our society measures equality in terms of power. Since there are no women within the Church's hierarchy, it is argued, women are not treated equally within the Church. The recent media storm advocating a separation of biology from personhood sows further confusion. A person can be what he or she wants, it is asserted, irrespective of one's body and physicality.

These mistaken notions of personhood and power must be corrected in order to understand the Church's teaching on the priesthood. The person is a harmonious union of body and soul created by God; a person cannot conceive of himself apart from his body. The Church honors the mutual complementarity of the sexes that was stamped into our nature at creation. This complementarity requires man and woman to enter into the union of marriage to procreate. The biological differences between men and women are real, and on account of them social and behavioral differences follow; the most obvious is motherhood and fatherhood. The old expression, "men are from Mars and women are from Venus," humorously encapsulates a fact societal forces have been moving against: men and women are different.

Differences in being do result in differences in treatment and expectation, even if we do not always realize that. A fifteen-year old and a five-year old in the same family are treated differently owing to their age. Likewise, within the same company a salesperson and a compliance officer have different roles: one must reach a sales quota, the other must track company protocols. So when their respective performances are reviewed by their employer, they are not subject to the same standards.

Properly understood, these differences are not a result of *ability*, but *capacity*. No one would call a five-year old unintelligent because he cannot read at the level of his fifteen-year old sister. Nor would anyone reasonably label a compliance officer a bad salesperson when she never had any training in that field. Rather, the five-year old is properly understood according to his potential as a five-year old, and the compliance officer is justly evaluated according to the particular standards of the compliance industry, not of any other.

Even though there are differences in the capacities of individuals, there is a greater unity that binds them together. The fifteen-year old and five-year old may be subject to differing expectations, but they are both loved equally by their parents, not because of what they can do, but because of who they are: children of mom and dad. The salesperson and compliance officer are evaluated differently due to their respective jobs, yet they are subject to the same code of conduct as fellow employees, and they are subject to the same lawful respect by their bosses.

From these examples we can better understand the Church's reservation of the priesthood to men only. The Church exists to serve all people, as all are equally worthy of Christ's redemption by virtue of their creation by God. Hence the Church treats all people with an equal dignity, and, despite occasional failures throughout her history, we regularly see the Church put this theory into action by her tireless advocacy for the most vulnerable persons among us: the unborn, the poor, the elderly, the sick, the dying.

To be clear, the priesthood is not reserved for men on the assumption that men have the ability and women do not. What we have experienced in recent decades dispels that notion immediately. Men are priests for their capacity to be configured to act in Christ's very person, and masculinity is an essential aspect of his personhood. Christ, the eternal High Priest of God the Father, offered himself on the Cross for our salvation. The Catholic priest stands at the altar to offer Christ's once-and-for-all sacrifice for us, and in doing so, he stands in the person of Christ, as if he were momentarily Christ.

Why the priesthood is reserved to men only is also based on the practice initiated by Christ, who chose only men to be his apostles. Jesus' actions during his ministry, whether in dealing with women or with the Jewish customs of the day, were never determined by societal expectations. This fact provides further reason to see deliberate intention on Christ's part in choosing only men to be priests.[17]

It is often remarked that the Church has changed over the centuries in response to the needs of a given age. This, without question, is true. Nevertheless, the Church has always tried to maintain what was said and done deliberately by Christ, even if the outward appearances surrounding these core teachings and actions have changed. This includes the sacraments, whose accompanying rituals have changed over the centuries but whose core elements—the specific matter chosen by Christ as bread, wine, water, and so on, as well as the specific prayers associated with them—have remained, and must remain, the same.

Because governing authority within the Church is inherently tied to holy orders, women cannot hold the office of bishop, priest, or pastor of a parish. This does not mean that women are forbidden from assisting bishops and priests in the task of governance. Increasing numbers of women are doing exactly this, serving as diocesan chancellors, theological advisors, and parish council members. Catholics must avoid viewing this

---

17. John Paul II, Apostolic Letter on Reserving Priestly Ordination to Men Alone, *Ordinatio Sacerdotalis* (May 22, 1994), 2. Vatican website: *www.vatican.va.*

structure as one of subordination, as the world wants to view it. Again, the varying roles within the Church are due to capacity, not ability, and not possessing particular capacities does not imply inferiority, just as the five-year old is not inferior to his fifteen-year old sister within the family, nor is the salesperson inferior to the compliance officer within the company.

Every call to service within the Church is a gift. In the natural order, we should not become upset when a sibling or friend receives a gift and we do not. We should maintain the same attitude within the Church, for not all of us are given the same gifts. We must pray for the humility to accept that reality, rather than let envy overcome us. Countless problems in Church history could have been avoided if more clergy and more lay people had chosen humility over envy.

Though not part of the hierarchy, women are essential members of the Church, and their dignity as persons is equal to that of any layman, priest, or bishop. The Church teaches that "the greatest in the Kingdom of Heaven are not the ministers but the saints."[18] The Church upholds countless woman saints as models of virtue for all Catholics to

---

18. Congregation for the Doctrine of the Faith, Declaration *Inter Insigniores* on the Question of the Admission of Women to the Ministerial Priesthood (October 15, 1976), 6. Vatican website: *www.vatican.va.* Quoted in John Paul II, *Ordinatio Sacerdotalis*, 3.

esteem and emulate, and there is no one whom the Church holds in higher regard than the Blessed Virgin Mary. Her name appears before the apostles in the Eucharistic prayers of the Mass, and more churches, prayers, and feast days across the world are dedicated to her than to any other saint. It is not to St. Peter or to St. Paul, nor any other pope or bishop, but to Mary alone that we address this praise: "You are the highest honor of our race."[19] No man is the father of God, but Mary is the mother of God according to the flesh. She had the sublime privilege of carrying the Son of God in her womb, and to him she gave her own flesh and blood. She, alone among human beings, was so exalted as to be preserved free from original sin by a singular act of God's favor. She, and no one else, was lifted body and soul into heaven at the end of her life.

The Catholic priesthood and the episcopacy's credibility have been undermined by actions committed by a few of their members. On the one hand, to implicate every priest and bishop as guilty by association would be to yield to the cynicism of our age, an attitude that is symptomatic of society's loss of faith. We would be wrong to lose faith in the priesthood or in the episcopacy as institutions, for they are the direct property of Christ himself who acts through

---

19. Responsorial Psalm for the Feast of Our Lady of Guadalupe, taken from Jud 13:18.

them. "God writes straight with crooked lines," goes the common saying. On the other hand, the faithful rightfully want to see reforms made such as safe environments, more effective screening of seminarians, and episcopal accountability. But since these actions demonstrated a deeper crisis of faith, only a deeper spiritual life among clergy and lay faithful alike will effectively salve the wounds.

If we heed the advice of another humble saint, Francis of Assisi, the people of God united as the Body of Christ can begin to heal. The first step is recalling the priest's divinely-bestowed task, and the incredible powers that are worked through him.

> We must also frequently visit churches and venerate and revere the clergy not so much for themselves, if they are sinners, but because of their office and administration of the most holy Body and Blood of Christ which they sacrifice upon the altar, receive and administer to others. And let all of us know for certain that no one can be saved except through the holy words and Blood of our Lord Jesus Christ which the clergy pronounce, proclaim, and minister. And they alone must minister and not others.[20]

---

20. Francis of Assisi, "Second Letter to the Faithful," in *Francis of Assisi—The Saint: Early Documents*, Vol. 1, ed. Armstrong, et al. (New York: New City Press, 2002), 47–48.

Francis continues,

> Blessed is the servant of God who has faith in the clergy who live uprightly according to the rite of the Holy Roman Church. Woe to those who look down upon them; for even though they be sinners, no one should judge them because the Lord alone reserves judgment on them to himself.[21]

The invisible God communicates his grace through visible signs. Only with the eyes of faith can we see that Jesus of Nazareth is God, that the Church has Christ as her head, that the sacraments communicate God's grace directly to our souls. We also need faith to see that the priest and the bishop act in the person of Christ. With the help of the Curé of Ars, St. John Vianney, we can begin to recall that the priesthood is really an exalted vocation, because it makes a man, though unworthy, a bridge between God and his people.

> What is a priest! A man who holds the place of God—a man who is invested with all the powers of God. . . . When the priest remits sins, he does not say, "God pardons you"; he says, "I absolve you." At

21. Francis of Assisi, "Admonition 26," in *Francis of Assisi—The Saint*, 136.

the Consecration, he does not say, "This is the Body of the Lord"; he says, "This is my body."

St. Bernard tells us that everything has come to us through Mary; and we may also say that everything has come to us through the priest; yes, all happiness, all graces, all heavenly gifts. If we had not the Sacrament of Orders, we should not have Our Lord. Who placed him there, in that tabernacle? It was the priest. What was it that received your soul, on its entrance into life? The priest. Who nourishes it, to give it strength to make its pilgrimage? The priest. Who will prepare it to appear before God, by washing the soul, for the last time, in the blood of Jesus Christ. The priest—always the priest.[22]

22. John Vianney, *The Little Catechism of The Curé of Ars* (Rockford, Illinois: TAN Books and Publishers, Inc., 1987), 33–34.

5

Why so many teachings?

We have seen that teachers function as bridges between a person seeking knowledge and knowledge itself. The Greek philosopher Aristotle, one of history's keenest observers of human nature, noted that "all men by nature desire to know."[1] Our immediate reactions to answer a ringing phone, text message, or knock at the door, and our eager inquiries after news, prove Aristotle correct. We want to know. And, naturally, we want our knowledge to be true.

Knowledge of God is the same. We want to have certitude that what we believe is true. Without certitude there is no reason to believe. So, if God made a definitive revelation of his Son who promised to be with us forever, it follows that he would establish an authority to ensure that this revelation remained intact.

1. Aristotle, *Metaphysics*, 980a, in *The Basic Works of Aristotle*, ed. Richard McKeon (New York: Random House, 1941).

In the words of St. John Henry Newman, "a revelation is not given, if there be no authority to decide what it is that is given."[2]

The Church's Magisterium is that authority, and it is possessed by the pope and the bishops in union with him. The Magisterium teaches with the authority of Christ, who gave the apostles, and, in turn, their successors, the power to continue his mission on earth. The content of their authoritative teaching is the deposit of faith, the single revelation of God that is alive within the Church. This single deposit comprises all that God revealed in the Old Testament, the teachings and works of Jesus Christ, and the preaching of the apostles.

According to the Second Vatican Council, the Magisterium has four functions:

> This teaching office is not above the word of God, but serves it, *teaching* only what has been handed on, *listening* to it devoutly, *guarding* it scrupulously and *explaining* it faithfully in accord with a divine commission and with the help of the Holy Spirit.[3]

---

2. John Henry Newman, *An Essay on the Development of Christian Doctrine* (Notre Dame, Indiana: University of Notre Dame Press, 1989), 89.

3. *Dei Verbum,* 10. Emphasis added.

The Magisterium, as the servant of God's Word, has no teaching of its own. It teaches only what it has received from Christ, which is the deposit of faith, and no more.

God's revelation to us closed with the death of the last apostle. Since then, the Church, in imitation of Mary, "kept all these things, pondering them in her heart" (Lk 2:19) through prayerful meditation on the deposit and through the pious living of her saints.[4] As a result the Church's insight into the deposit has deepened and developed through the centuries so that the Magisterium has come to articulate more precisely the many facets of the mystery of salvation. Every formal teaching must have roots in the mystery of salvation as conveyed through the Bible and the living tradition of the Church. The Magisterium does not, and cannot, invent new teachings, nor can it adapt or change old teachings in such a way that continuity is broken between the old and the new.

For example, today we understand the angel's declaration of Mary—"Hail, full of grace, the Lord is with you" (Lk 1:28)—as the evidence for Mary's immaculate conception free from original sin, which is the state deprived of grace. The theology of the Immaculate Conception is a deeper understanding, on a rational level,

4. John Henry Newman, *Oxford Sermon 15*, 3.

of St. Luke's formulation, and it took nearly 1,800 years before it was definitively taught by the Magisterium.

Because of this organic development of God's teachings from a single revelation, there is an inherent unity in all the Church's teachings. From this one revelation comes the Church's teachings on God, creation, Jesus Christ, salvation, sacraments, morality, and prayer. Together all the teachings form a single body with God as their source, just as the Church is a single body with Christ as her head. To believe one particular teaching is to believe all of them, and to reject one is essentially to reject all of them.

As the Church's teaching authority, the Magisterium's task is to present the mysteries of faith in ways we can more readily understand. The primary vehicles for transmitting the Faith are dogmas, infallible statements of what we believe as Catholics. Dogmas form the core of Catholic doctrine, or teaching, and are presented together in narrative form in a creed. The Nicene Creed we recite each Sunday at Mass narrates the most essential dogmas of our Faith. Other dogmas include the real presence of Christ in the Eucharist, the foundation of the Church and the seven sacraments by Christ, the primacy of St. Peter and his successors over the Universal Church, and Mary's status as the mother of God, along with her immaculate conception, perpetual virginity, and bodily assumption.

Catholic dogmas invite us to contemplate the great mysteries of salvation. In doing so they point us to Christ who is the living embodiment of dogma. Dogmas are necessary, explains St. John Henry Newman, because our finite minds cannot comprehend these mysteries except in piecemeal form.[5] This is one reason why the Church has so many teachings: inexhaustible realities have manifold implications, and all of them must be presented as the many parts of God's single revelation for us to grasp their full meaning. At the same time, it is necessary to delineate what is part of these mysteries and what is distortion. Dogmas protect the faithful from being deceived by the latter, functioning akin to the foul lines in baseball; they tell us what is of the mystery and what is not. In other words, dogmas are truths revealed by God and taught by the Church.

We also must not forget, warns Newman, that behind all dogmatic expressions are infinite realities:

> Catholic dogmas are, after all, but symbols of Divine fact, which, far from being compassed by those very propositions, would not be exhausted nor fathomed by a thousand.[6]

5. John Henry Newman, *Oxford Sermon*, 23.

6. John Henry Newman, *Oxford Sermon*, 23.

Dogmas are infallibly taught, but they remain human formulations of divine events. They are, to use an image from St. Thomas Aquinas, mere straw compared to the divine realities they convey.

Because of their inherent connections to the divine, dogmas bring gifts to our spiritual lives. Far from inhibiting personal faith, dogmas inspire personal reflection and growth in the life of faith. Hence the *Catechism* teaches that

> dogmas are lights along the path of faith; they illuminate it and make it secure. Conversely, if our life is upright, our intellect and heart will be open to welcome the light shed by the dogmas of faith.[7]

By illuminating the path of faith, dogmas also serve as spurs for evangelization and for Christian charity.

Dogmas form the core of the Magisterium's teaching because they express the "main events," so to speak, of God's revelation to us. In other words, dogmas are statements that God wants his people to know. The specific content of dogmas is "what is to be believed in faith and applied in practice," or, as more commonly called, matters of faith and morals.[8] In the words of the *Catechism*,

---

7. *CCC*, 89.

8. Avery Dulles, *Magisterium: Teacher and Guardian of the Faith* (Naples, Florida: Sapientia Press, 2007), 63.

> the moral law finds its fullness and its unity in Christ. Jesus Christ is in person the way of perfection. He is the end of the law, for only he teaches and bestows the justice of God.[9]

The moral law taught by the Church is grounded in the natural law, which, as mentioned in Chapter 2, enables human beings to discern good from evil through the faculty of reason innate in us all. The *Catechism* teaches that observance of the natural law is necessary for salvation.[10]

Since the natural law is discerned through reason, it is accessible to all people, not just Catholics. Yet God has complemented every one of these natural law precepts with the Ten Commandments, which present three positive norms (worship God alone, keep holy the sabbath, honor thy father and mother) and seven negative norms to be avoided. The negative norms, be they expressed through natural law or revealed, are infallibly taught by the Church because they concern actions that are intrinsically evil, that is, always wrong in every circumstance,[11] be they murder, adultery, or theft.

There is a hierarchy of Church teachings, the full panoply of which can be likened to a tree. The Old

---

9. *CCC*, 1953.

10. *CCC*, 2036.

11. Dulles, *Magisterium: Teacher and Guardian of the Faith*, 80.

Testament forms the tree's roots that reach deep into the soil. The mystery of Christ and the life he calls us to, as articulated in the Church's dogmas on faith and morals, form the tree trunk—the solid foundation of belief. These articles of faith articulate the very reason for the Church's existence. Theologians call these infallible dogmas "primary object truths."

Growing from the trunk are thick tree limbs so closely connected to the trunk that they cannot be separated. These "limbs" carry the theological name of "secondary object truths," and they are infallibly taught because of their closeness to the trunk, that is, to revelation itself. The Church has consistently articulated these points throughout her history. These teachings include the aforementioned moral prohibitions derived from the natural law, the canonization of saints, and the authority of an ecumenical council of bishops deliberating in union with the pope. These are teachings we hold as Catholics because they are necessary consequences of what we believe.

From these limbs extend numerous other branches that are corollaries of these teachings. They may be articulations of a dogma's consequences, such as the need to show the utmost reverence to the Holy Eucharist because of Christ's Real Presence within it; or they may be practical applications of dogmatic teaching intended to direct us at a specific point in history, such as teachings on bioethics and governments. Further removed from the trunk, these teachings are not considered, nor were they ever intended to be, infallible. They are not straight explanations of revelation as dogmas are, but teachings with an eye toward directing temporal affairs. Such teachings run the gamut from the effects the sacraments have on us to the Church's social teachings that touch on the economy, working conditions, and the environment. Though not infallible, these teachings are still authoritatively taught with the expectation that members of the Body of Christ will accept them with trust. We will consider the response of the faithful to the Magisterium's teachings in more detail below.

The Magisterium has a specified means by which it delivers its different teachings. There are two modes of teaching, the extraordinary mode and ordinary mode. Because of the incredible importance of dogma as authoritative statements of God's own revelation, dogma is normally defined in the extraordinary mode. There are then two ways in which the Magisterium exercises this extraordinary mode of teaching.

The first way is through an ecumenical council, a solemn gathering of the bishops from all over the world in union with the pope who together define a teaching as a dogma. The Nicene Creed, as mentioned, is one example of a narrative statement of several dogmas defined at the Church's first ecumenical council in Nicaea (modern day Turkey) in 325. Later councils defined as dogmas the nature of the Trinity, the reality and transmission of original sin, and the existence of purgatory, among others.

There have been twenty-one ecumenical councils in the Church's history, and nearly all of them have defined dogmas, with the Second Vatican Council being an exception. Not every teaching and document produced by a council is a dogma, however. When a dogma is defined, it is done so solemnly. Again, dogmatic statements are limited to the matters of faith and morals that the Church is certain to have been revealed by God.

The second manner of extraordinary teaching is when the pope, exercising his authority as the successor of St. Peter and leader of the Universal Church, defines a teaching as an infallible dogma. The ability of the pope to do so was itself defined as a dogma by the First Vatican Council in 1870, and this was an articulated development of the authority Christ gave to St. Peter. In the modern era the pope has only issued two infallible teachings in this manner: once to proclaim Mary's immaculate conception, and the second time to declare Mary's bodily assumption into heaven.

So often the papal mode of extraordinary teaching is subject to misunderstanding. The pope as a man is not infallible, nor are the decisions he makes as pope. The charism of infallibility protects the pope's teaching from error when he specifically invokes his authority as Peter's successor and head of the Universal Church to proclaim an absolute teaching on faith and morals for all the faithful to hold.[12] To define a teaching in this way is not to bring the pope more worldly esteem, but to give certitude to the faithful that what the pope is proclaiming has been revealed by God, and not merely taught by human beings.

The ordinary mode of the Magisterium's teaching also is used in two ways, and these are far more common than their extraordinary mode counterparts. One way is the Magisterium of the pope as expressed in his homilies, public speeches, letters, and encyclicals. Through all these means, the pope teaches the deposit of faith, first, by reiterating it in language suited for the present moment; second, by applying its implications to address contemporary problems; or third, by affirming what the Church has always taught. The first two cannot be taught infallibly because of their temporal nature; they are intended not to be eternally valid but limited to guide a given age. The third is infallible according to the pope's ordinary teaching authority because he is confirming, in

12. *Lumen Gentium,* 25.

the words of St. Vincent of Lérins, the "faith which has been believed everywhere, always, by all."[13]

Examples of infallible teachings according to the pope's ordinary Magisterium include the reservation of the priesthood to men, as well as the immorality of abortion, euthanasia, and artificial birth control. Rather than pronounce a solemn definition, teaching infallibly via the ordinary Magisterium underscores that the teaching does not belong to a particular pope, but to the constant teaching of the Church.

The second manner of ordinary teaching is when the bishops in union with the pope unanimously present for the faithful an aspect of the deposit of faith. Examples include homilies and pastoral letters that proclaim God's Incarnation at Christmas or the need for repentance during Lent. Such teachings manifest the catholicity of the Church and her union with the successor of St. Peter. When individual bishops teach the deposit of faith within their own diocese and apply it to meet the needs of their people, they are not protected by the charism of infallibility. They nonetheless remain the authoritative teachers within their diocese by virtue of their office.

13. Vincent of Lérins, *Commonitorium* 2.6, in *Nicene and Post-Nicene Fathers, Second Series*, Vol. 11, ed. Philip Schaff and Henry Wace, trans. C.A. Heurtley (Buffalo, NY: Christian Literature Publishing Co., 1894), 567.

Through these teachings, Catholics hear an authentic witness of Jesus Christ.

It is all too easy to become caught up in the technicalities of Church teaching, to become consumed by the nature of infallibility, to debate obsessively how authoritative individual teachings may be. These distinctions are not unimportant, and they exist because the mysteries that they expound are so incredibly precious. Yet we cannot forget that these levels of teaching ought to be understood together as expressions of God's singular revelation as spoken through his eternal Word, Jesus Christ.

Heresy: A Real Danger

Jesus knew the weakness of the men whom he ordained to teach his gospel. It is no wonder, then, that he who is infallible in his very person would provide a means whereby his infallible Word could remain such, even when preached by fallible men. In inviting us to trust him, Jesus also invites us to trust the means he established to guide us to him—the Church and her Magisterium.

Deliberate distortions of the deposit of faith are heresies, which typically develop when a person overemphasizes one aspect of the Faith while denying a corollary. For instance, early heresies about the person of Jesus conflated his divine or his human nature; one nature was overemphasized while the other was intentionally denied. The Protestant heresies of the sixteenth century were similar: rather than keep faith and works, Scripture and Tradition, as complementary pairs, faith and Scripture were exalted while works and Tradition were rejected.

Too often in Church history, we have seen bishops and priests succumb to heresy. The powers of ordination do not make a man free from sin, nor do they make him fully docile to the Church; among the most infamous heretics in history, Nestorius was a bishop, Martin Luther and Arius were priests. These three are extreme examples, as each developed his own theology to rival that of the Church. A more subtle, and more common, heresy occurs when bishops or priests deny a teaching of the Church, and instruct the faithful that it is permissible for them to do so as well. In recent decades this latter form of heresy has been dangerously prevalent in some Catholic schools and among some priests in denying the Church's ability to teach infallibly on morals, especially those pertaining to human sexuality.

Bishops and priests whose personal teachings depart from those of the Church retain their governing authority by virtue of their respective offices. But the faithful are not obliged to heed any teaching that deviates from the deposit of faith, which all the clergy are supposed to teach in its fullness. When the faithful reasonably believe that a bishop or priest is teaching something contrary to the deposit of faith, they have the duty to approach him with charity to work for clarification, and, if found to be necessary, rectification. In this they ought to follow the counsel of St. Ignatius Loyola:

> Every good Christian ought to be more willing to give a good interpretation to the statement of another than to condemn it as false. If he cannot give a good interpretation to this statement, he should ask the other how he understands it, and if he is in error, he should correct it. If this is not sufficient, he should seek every suitable means of correcting his understanding so that he may be saved from error.[14]

Because of our culture's skepticism of religious truth, it is tempting to dismiss concerns of orthodoxy—that is, correct belief—as trivial, divisive, or irrelevant to Catholic living. Insistence on orthodoxy, it is alleged, has caused many religious wars that could have been avoided. When this thesis combines with the

---

14. Ignatius of Loyola, *The Spiritual Exercises of St. Ignatius*, trans. Anthony Mottola (New York: Image Books, 1964), 47.

oft-heard presumption that God does not care about our religious rules, we have the reduction of faith to personal sentiment; it does not matter what we believe, but only what we do.

This is the wrong presumption. The profound unity of faith and morals—of belief and action—proves how critical correct belief is. Belief in God and acceptance of God's commandments have inspired some of history's bravest heroes, most incredible sacrifices, and the most awe-inspiring humanitarian and artistic achievements. By contrast, disbelief in God and incorrect beliefs about the human person have catalyzed history's most horrific atrocities.

Orthodoxy matters. To love Jesus Christ we must know him. To know him we must learn the full truth about him and everything he wants us to know and do as his followers. Christ endowed his Church with special gifts to be sure that we know him, and not distortions of him. To know him, then, we must have faith in his Church's supernatural powers that transcend her natural limitations, and not think that we know better.

The Faithful's Reception of Church Teaching

Although the Church has a governing structure, its government is not that of a nation, whose government protects a people's ability to live freely within a given territory. Since the Church was founded not by any human being, but by Jesus Christ, her authority comes not from the consent of the people, but from God. Members come by God's invitation to form a single body with Christ as its head, and they therefore profess together one Lord, one Faith, and one baptism.

There is a tension, then, between the message of modernity, with its emphasis on personal choice, and the expectations of the Church, which Cardinal Avery Dulles aptly identifies:

> People who live in a free democratic society have difficulty in understanding why they ought to submit their minds to a Magisterium. They often fail to understand the distinctiveness of the Church as a community of faith. Membership in the Church, unlike membership in secular societies, depends upon sharing the beliefs of the community. Christ equipped the Church with a hierarchical Magisterium that has the competence to articulate what the members should believe to keep them united among themselves and, most importantly, united to their divine Teacher. The Magisterium should be seen not as a burden but as a gift and a blessing.[15]

---

15. Dulles, *Magisterium: Teacher and Guardian of the Faith*, 99.

Unity within the body is critical. Analogously, for a football team to succeed there must be unity among the players. They must share the same goal of winning, and they must share the same doctrine: the plays they practice each week and then call out in the huddle before each snap. If a player does not share the same goal as the team, he undermines it, even as he remains part of it. If a player rejects a particular offensive scheme for any reason, choosing instead to run his own play that differs from the one his coach designed and his other ten teammates are running, he impairs the team and himself. The team, now effectively outnumbered, has a more difficult time advancing the ball against the opposition. The breakaway player can hurt himself physically by running apart from his team's designs. And, consumed by pride, he can also hurt himself emotionally by allowing resentment to build up in his heart, thinking that his play was more effective, that his coach is wrong, that his teammates are foolish for obeying the coach's poorly-designed play. Should this player express to his teammates and coach his frustration in an accusatory, rather than inquiring, manner, the other members may be provoked to anger. Needless to say, with dissent raging within team ranks, it becomes much more difficult for the players to play good football and achieve their goal. The key for team success is trust—in one's teammates, one's coach, and in the team plan.

The same goes for the team that is the people of God united as the Body of Christ. The members of the body must trust God, first and foremost, and, as a consequence, trust the Magisterium that God gave us to pass on his revelation. They must trust the presence of the Holy Spirit within the Church that keeps the Magisterium from error when pronouncing on faith and morals. And they must trust that particular teachings that may appear confusing, challenging, or contrary to one's personal desires are in fact correct and worthy of embracing.

We see the rationale, then, for why Catholics are obliged, in the words of the Second Vatican Council, to give "loyal submission of the will and intellect" to the infallible teachings of the Church, and to accept with reverence other temporal teachings that are not infallible.[16] In other words, the faithful are called to obey the Magisterium's teachings and to accept these teachings as true; these are actions of the will and intellect, respectively.

Just like the breakaway football player, a Catholic who rejects one or more teachings causes harm both to the Church and to himself. The body is weakened each time a member turns against it. Surely the Church's witness

16. *Lumen Gentium,* 25.

to the world is not as effective when some of her members are denying her doctrine. The individual, because he rejects an aspect of Church teaching, no longer feels as closely connected to his figurative teammates as he would if he accepted everything. He can hurt himself spiritually by refusing to live according to the Church's guidance, and resentment toward the Church can build in his heart on account of his differing opinion. Communion between him and the body, and, as a result, between him and Christ the head of the Church, languishes.

When the secular world frames the discussion about religion, it deliberately places the individual believer at odds with the Church, attempting to make the Church bow to the will of the individual. "Which teachings do I want to believe?" goes the argument, as if each of us can pick and choose as we wish. The correct approach is the opposite, and begins from a position of faith:

> I believe that Jesus Christ founded a Church and sent the Holy Spirit to ensure his teachings reach me uncorrupted. Hence, I believe everything that the Church teaches, and I try to live by these teachings, out of obedience to Christ whom I have been called to love and serve.

To maintain this humble openness is to think with the Church—*sentire cum ecclesia*, as it is known.

We should not be troubled if difficulties with Church teachings, or with faith in God, occasionally seize us. First, our intellects are finite, and concupiscence can cloud our ability to perceive the truth. Second, inherent within the life of faith is a natural unrest,[17] for, even as we believe, God's invisibility can unsettle us, just as we can feel when we travel to a new state and worry whether we are in the correct location. Like Peter when he walked on water, the drama of faith includes learning to trust that God will keep us afloat even when we encounter stormy seas. The nature of faith, by contrast, *invites* us to *accept* what God has revealed to us through his Church. To accept God is an act of freedom, not coercion, and God makes it possible by sending grace to help us choose.

No one is a "bad Catholic" for having questions or difficulties about Church teachings. Quite the contrary: our natural desire to understand makes us inquire into the teachings' inner logic, which may not be readily apparent to our intellects, especially when these teachings are contested by others. If we have difficulties during our inquiry, we appeal to faith—to faith seeking understanding. With faith in the Church as our starting point, we can then seek the counsel of others and pray

---

17. Joseph Pieper, *Faith, Hope, Love* (San Francisco: Ignatius Press, 1997), 50–53.

that the Holy Spirit may enlighten our intellects with his grace, so that we can understand on a rational level what we know on the level of faith to be true.

To have difficulties with Church teaching is not the same thing as doubting it. Doubt is the opposite of faith, for it withholds trust from another person and his testimony. St. John Henry Newman has articulated the difference between difficulty and doubt better than anyone:

> Ten thousand difficulties do not make one doubt . . . difficulty and doubt are incommensurate. There of course may be difficulties in the evidence . . . A man may be annoyed that he cannot work out a mathematical problem, of which the answer is or is not given to him, without doubting that it admits of an answer, or that a certain particular answer is the true one.[18]

With faith in Christ and his Church, we will receive grace to overcome any difficulties we may encounter.

As members of the body, God aids his people collectively in accepting his revelation with a "supernatural appreciation of the faith," known by its Latin name of the *sensus fidei*.[19] The *sensus fidei* is a gift of the

---

18. *Apologia Pro Vita Sua* (New York: Penguin Classics, 1994), 214–215.

19. *Lumen Gentium,* 12.

Holy Spirit that enables the whole body of the faithful, when and only when it is united with the bishops and pope, to assent to the teaching of the Magisterium without error. The *sensus fidei* was at work, for example, when the faithful received the proclamations of Mary's immaculate conception and assumption as dogmas in 1854 and 1950, respectively, with great joy across the globe.

The *sensus fidei* is not a public opinion poll among believers. Public opinion, cautions Cardinal Dulles, "may be correct, but it often reflects the tendencies of our fallen human nature, the trends of the times, and the pressures of public media."[20] Rather, the *sensus fidei* is a grace that opens the faithful to receiving the correct teaching of the Church, and it "is generally more acute in proportion to their personal faith and holiness."[21]

Through the light of faith, we learn that the Church's teachings, which are Christ's own, bring a yoke that is easy, and a burden that is light, because they point us to the truth of our very being. When we know that we are on the path of truth, feelings of obligation are replaced by those of joy, since "truth is not

---

20. Dulles, *Magisterium: Teacher and Guardian of the Faith*, 45.

21. Dulles, *Magisterium: Teacher and Guardian of the Faith*, 44.

an abstract idea, but is Jesus himself, the Word of God in whom is the Life that is the Light of man, the Son of God who is also the Son of Man."[22] God has a plan for each of us to encounter his Son and live out his truth. To this plan we now turn.

22. Francis, Apostolic Constitution on Ecclesiastical Universities and Faculties, *Veritatis Gaudium* (January 29, 2018), 1. Vatican website: *press.vatican.va*.

6

My Role in the Church?

The specific roles of lay men and lay women, who are the Church's non-ordained members, are essential, even if these roles are not immediately obvious. If we did not know better, the situation on any given Sunday, with one priest offering the Mass and hundreds of lay people watching him, could give credence to the cynical comment sometimes batted about: that the job of the laity is "to pray, pay, and obey."

There is truth to this comment. Prayer is foundational to our lives as Catholics, and we are called to obey the commandments of God and the precepts of the Church as delivered by the hierarchy. But this caricature might lead one to think that the laity's role is confined to the four walls of a church building. This is not the case.

The Second Vatican Council teaches that lay men and women are to "seek the kingdom of God by engaging temporal affairs and directing them according to

God's will."[1] In the workplace, the park, the gym, and the home, the laity "contribute to the sanctification of the world, as from within like leaven, by fulfilling their own particular duties."[2] In other words, the vocation of the laity is to sanctify the world in two ways: by sharing Christ with whomever they meet and by performing their particular tasks in life for God's glory. Both ways are open-ended, allowing for creativity in how we reach the goal.

In general, the first way the laity sanctifies the world—by sharing Christ with whomever we meet—is exercised in the parish, in the workplace, or with our family and friends. Sharing Christ with others has two names: evangelization, which places the accent on communicating Christ's gospel to others; or apostolate, which refers to a specific activity through which a person brings Christ to others. In the parish all lay men and women evangelize simply by attending Mass each week and supporting their fellow parishioners by their presence, prayer, and good will.

Sharing Christ in the workplace or within the extended family is a much more formidable challenge than in the parish, which has a self-selecting constituency

1. *Lumen Gentium*, 31.

2. *Lumen Gentium*, 31.

for its activities. In both the workplace and the family, by contrast, we find people indifferent or even hostile to Christ and to the Catholic Faith.

To share Christ in these environments, we first must pray for courage so we can overcome our natural reluctance and fear of rejection. We then have two ways of proceeding. One is to open an individual conversation with someone who we think may be open to Christ's message, or who, seemingly downtrodden, could benefit from the hope that faith in Christ brings. Before we speak, we must pray to the Holy Spirit for inspiration, asking him to guide our minds and spark the most appropriate words for the situation. In doing so we have Jesus' pledge of support: "Do not worry about how you are to defend yourselves or what you are to say; for the Holy Spirit will teach you at that very hour what you ought to say" (Lk 12:11–12).

There is no question that increasing numbers of people are moving away from the Church.[3] If we wish to reverse that trend, we each have to overcome our reticence and carry out the command of Jesus: "Go into all the world and proclaim the good news to the whole creation" (Mk 16:15). From the time of the first martyrs

3. Pew Research Center, "In U.S., Decline of Christianity Continues at a Rapid Pace," October 17, 2019.

to our own day, the best case for Catholicism remains the personal witness of those devoted to Christ and his Church. If we do so, we could be God's chosen impetus for a lonely soul who has been silently crying out for salvation. After all, none of us would have the gift of faith if it had not been for someone inviting us to it.

Among our family members, friends, and co-workers who are more resistant to religion, there is another, more subtle, manner of sharing Christ with them. Rather than engage them directly in conversation, we can carry out our duties with resolve and maintain a disposition worthy of a Christian disciple: we try to keep a joyful demeanor as much as possible, we do the work assigned to us honestly and diligently, we limit our complaints, we refrain from gossip and swearing, we treat everyone with kindness, we silently say grace before eating our meals.

These are simple, practical ways whereby, following the advice of St. Theresa of Calcutta, we can do small things with great love. In acting in this way, we do not wear our faith on our sleeve. Rather, as the French philosopher Étienne Gilson explains, we act as

> Catholics who would make Catholicism so enter into their everyday lives and work that the unbelieving would come to wonder what secret force animated

that work and that life, and that, having discovered
it, they would say to the themselves, on the contrary:
he is a very good man, and now I know why: it is
because he is a Catholic.[4] *— Good is our Spirit*
St Augustin—We are spiritual beings having human experience

In addition to witnessing to individuals, we are also
called to sanctify institutions, schools, governments, and
the wider culture. On the one hand, we have a duty to
confront sin, evil, or injustices that we know are wrong
and must be corrected. We cannot sit idle while evil realities take root in our culture. The Second Vatican Council gives clear instructions in this regard:

> By uniting their forces, let the laity so remedy the
> institutions and conditions of the world when the lat-
> ter are an inducement to sin, that these may be con-
> formed to the norms of justice, favoring rather than
> hindering the practice of virtue.[5]

On the other hand, even healthy institutions can benefit from an infusion of holiness from within their ranks.
The council continues,

> By so doing they will impregnate culture and human
> works with a moral value. In this way the field of the

4. Étienne Gilson, "The Intelligence in the Service of Christ the King,"
in *Christianity and Philosophy* (New York: Sheed & Ward, 1939), 118.

5. *Lumen Gentium,* 36.

> world is better prepared for the seed of the divine word and the doors of the Church are opened more widely through which the message of peace may enter the world.[6]

The opportunities are limitless and will arise spontaneously: we may need to resist inappropriate messages or programming for children, to notify the proper authorities of unjust activities, or to bring Catholic virtues into a secular environment.

It is natural to be uncomfortable or even intimidated by the thought of living our faith in the workplace and in the wider culture. Today a radical movement of secularization has duped most into thinking that religion is a purely private matter that should be confined to the home and to church buildings; it must not be brought into the public arena, it is asserted. This claim is wrong and emanates from anti-religious prejudice. Catholics know that a society flourishes when its people and institutions espouse a genuinely Christian way of living.

Certainly, we are not the first lay Catholics to face hostility for living our faith in the workplace. For inspiration, we can turn to St. Thomas More (1477–1535)

---

6. *Lumen Gentium*, 36.

and St. Gianna Beretta Molla (1922–1962). Both are renowned for their heroic deaths. But their courage did not suddenly appear out of nowhere: it was the fruit of a profound love for God who provided them—as he provides us—the grace needed to live the Catholic Faith intentionally in the workplace.

Thomas More was an English lawyer who worked for the royal government almost his entire professional life. Elected to Parliament at age twenty-four, More immediately raised his voice to oppose King Henry VII's attempt to raise taxes to finance what More perceived as an unjust cause.[7] His courage brought the king's wrath upon him and his family; it also brought imprisonment and fines for More's father in reprisal.[8] More's outstanding work over the years prompted his promotion to a number of government and judicial posts. The famous Renaissance humanist Desiderius Erasmus, a friend of More's, commented that in judging civil cases

> no one has disposed of more cases than he nor acted with greater integrity; indeed, he usually remits the fee charged to litigants which is three shillings

7. James Monti, *The King's Good Servant But God's First* (San Francisco: Ignatius Press, 1997), 44.

8. James Monti, *The King's Good Servant But God's First*, 45.

deposited by each beforehand. By such conduct he has made himself much beloved in the city.[9]

When Gianna Beretta, born in Italy in 1922, sought to enroll in medical school, she faced opposition on two fronts: societal expectations that were hostile to women becoming doctors, and the Second World War, which forced her to study not in Milan as she desired, but in the safer town of Pavia.[10] Gianna persevered and became a pediatrician so she could serve both children and their mothers.[11] And this she did: patients streamed to her office, where Gianna would allow them to pay her with eggs or chickens when money was still tight after the war.[12] At age thirty-three, Gianna married Pietro Molla, and the two began a family. She continued to practice medicine after her children

---

9. Quoted in E.E. Reynolds, *The Field Is Won: The Life and Death of Saint Thomas More* (Milwaukee: The Bruce Publishing Company, 1968), 70.

10. Brian O'Neel, *39 New Saints You Should Know* (Cincinnati: Servant Books, 2010), 38–39; Dexter Duggan, "St. Gianna's Final Sacrifice Well-Known . . . But What of Her Decades of Faith that Came Before?" *The Wanderer Press*, September 19, 2019.

11. Duggan, "St. Gianna's Final Sacrifice Well-Known . . . But What of Her Decades of Faith that Came Before?"

12. Duggan, "St. Gianna's Final Sacrifice Well-Known . . . But What of Her Decades of Faith that Came Before?"

were born, not for the money, but so she could bring Christ to her patients.[13] Doctors, she said, "are called to bring God into a situation where priests are not able to assist. . . . Whoever touches the body of a patient touches the body of Christ."[14]

When called by God to give their lives in the most severe test of their love for him, both More and Molla were able to draw strength from a lifetime of faith and charity, even as they each faced enormous pressure from their peers to acquiesce. In More's case, King Henry VIII had broken from the Catholic Church and forced his subjects to swear an oath of allegiance to him as head of the new Church of England. More, the second man to the king in governmental administration, refused—he knew that the Church belonged to Christ and not to any man, no matter how powerful. In April 1534, on account of his continued refusal, he was imprisoned in the Tower of London on a charge of treason. In the ensuing months the king personally sent emissaries to pressure More to acquiesce so he could save his life and his social position. Still, he refused. He was found guilty of treason in a rigged trial and was beheaded on July 6, 1535. Often called a martyr for conscience, Thomas More was also a

13. O'Neel, *39 New Saints You Should Know*, 40.

14. O'Neel, *39 New Saints You Should Know*, 40.

martyr for the Church as founded by Christ and led by his earthly vicar, the pope.

When pregnant with her fourth child in 1961, Dr. Gianna Beretta Molla was diagnosed with cancer. Her doctors recommended treatment that would, as a side effect, cause the death of her baby. She refused the treatment. As she went into the delivery room on Holy Saturday 1962, she told her husband, "If you must decide between me and the child, do not hesitate: choose the child—I insist on it. Save the baby."[15] Gianna gave birth to a healthy baby girl, but she immediately suffered an infection that quickly spread through her cancer-weakened body.[16] Knowing that she would not survive, she asked to be brought home. Gianna died a week later, making the words of Jesus her own: "Greater love has no man than this, that a man lay down his life for his friends" (Jn 15:3).

Precious few of us are called to give the ultimate sacrifice for living our Faith as More and Molla did. Yet we can take away two lessons from their witness. First, in order to be a witness for others, we each must cultivate our own personal holiness. This does not require a semi-miraculous act on our part, but the willing pursuit

15. O'Neel, *39 New Saints You Should Know*, 41.

16. O'Neel, *39 New Saints You Should Know*, 41.

of the Church's ingredients for holiness: the Mass, daily prayer, the sacrament of reconciliation, reading the Bible and other spiritual reading. Such activities transform us not in one fell swoop, but gradually over time, as they help us imitate Christ our Lord and the source of all grace. Second, we learn that authentic holiness requires us to die to ourselves in small ways, just as Christ admonished us:

> If any man would come after me, let him deny himself and take up his cross daily and follow me. For whoever would save his life will lose it; and whoever loses his life for my sake, he will save it. (Lk 9:23–24)

Living for God's Glory

The acts of More and Molla also bring us to the second way, in addition to bearing witness to Christ for the good of others, that lay men and women exercise their vocation in the world: by performing our particular tasks for God's glory. To work for God's glory does not require a grand stage or occupations that are religious in nature. It requires only one thing: that we consciously do whatever we must do—be it our professional occupations, our housework, our maintenance on our homes and cars, our driving our children to various places—with an eye toward pleasing God who charged us with these activities as part of our vocations in the world. We thus act as young children who cheerfully draw pictures simply to win their parents' approval. Children conceive images that they think will please their parents, they use multiple colors, and they pour themselves into their artwork. As children age, they seek the same goal, this time by trying to achieve in school and in extracurricular activities; they hope that by mastering their particular craft, they will make their parents happy and pleased with them. In other words, children carry out their normal activities with a goal external to the activity itself and perceived as greater than it.

The same goes for us on earth as we try to please our Father in heaven. We complete the tasks before us to the best of our ability according to their respective standards, realizing that if we do them as best we can, we glorify God who gave us these tasks. God is pleased with our honest efforts. If we are conscious of this fact while we work, we transform the work at our hands from an end in itself to a means whereby we are sanctified. In this way, like children working to please their parents, we, in the words of St. Josemaría Escrivá, "work with such supernatural vision that we let ourselves be absorbed by our activity only to make it divine. In this way the earthly becomes divine, the temporal eternal."[17]

17. Josemaría Escrivá, *The Forge* 730, in *The Way. Furrow. The Forge* (New York: Scepter Publishers, 2011), 755. Original in the second person.

We can do this with work of any type, from saving lives as an ocean lifeguard to changing diapers as a parent at home. Before Jesus began his public ministry, he lived an ordinary human life for thirty years, charged with the same mundane chores that we all still face today: maintaining the house, cleaning the floor, and earning a living through sweat and toil. St. Josemaría Escrivá explains that by living this simple life and performing manual labor, Jesus reveals "that human existence—your life—and its humdrum, ordinary business, have a meaning which is divine, which belongs to eternity."[18] All the work we do, be it our occupation or a particularly onerous task before us, has a greater purpose beyond itself. Each endeavor offers an occasion to work for God, simply by reminding ourselves that whatever we do in life, we do for him.

Ever conscious of how difficult it can be for us to overcome daily drudgery, the Church offers for our imitation saints who transformed their lives, and the lives of others, by carrying out mundane tasks with great love. St. André Bessette (1845–1937) of Canada is one of them. Orphaned at the age of twelve, young André did not receive a formal education because he had to work

---

18. Josemaría Escrivá, *The Forge* 730, in *The Way. Furrow. The Forge*, 688.

to support himself.[19] He entered the Congregation of the Holy Cross in the province of Québec and became a professed religious brother. Due to his lack of education and his poor health, he was assigned the job of porter, or doorkeeper, of Notre Dame College, where his duties included greeting guests, washing floors, cleaning lamps, and carrying firewood.[20] Yet Br. André realized that these seemingly menial tasks had a dignified place in God's hidden plan for our salvation: "It is with the smallest brushes that the artists paint the most beautiful pictures," he said.[21]

When guests came to the college, Br. André received them and prayed with them, entrusting their intentions to the intercession of St. Joseph, to whom he was deeply devoted. Br. André's sincere piety and humility inspired the guests, and some even experienced physical healings while praying with him. As his reputation for holiness grew, he constantly deflected the praise he received to St. Joseph's intercession. Br. André also gave haircuts to the students at the college for five cents; he used the collected money to build the Oratory of St.

---

19. St. André Bessette, Congregation of Holy Cross, *http://holycrosscongregation.org/holy-ones/st-andre-bessette.*

20. St. André Bessette, Catholic News Agency, *https://www.catholicnewsagency.com/saint/st-andre-bessette-732.*

21. St. André Bessette, Catholic News Agency.

Joseph in Montreal.[22] Praying with the sick who came, and maintaining this oratory which was eventually enlarged into a basilica to accommodate the multitude who kept visiting, became Br. André's work until his death at age ninety-one. When he died, over a million people came to see his body lying in state at the basilica, whose side altars were covered with the crutches of those who had been healed by Br. André's intercession.[23]

The story of St. André reminds us that our seemingly ordinary activities have eternal significance. The same goes for the struggles and sufferings we encounter over the course of our lives. With the eyes of faith, suffering, like work, carries eternal significance.

In the context of human suffering, our redemption takes on deeper meaning. God could have redeemed us—literally, bought us back—from sin in any manner he desired. He chose to do so by sending his Son to become one of us, so that he, too, could experience human suffering in all its agonies. He suffered unimaginable physical pain on the Cross; he suffered mental anguish knowing that he created those who were torturing him; he suffered morally in being rejected by his own people and abandoned by his closest friends; he

22. St. André Bessette, Congregation of Holy Cross.

23. St. André Bessette, Congregation of Holy Cross.

suffered spiritually, feeling as if God had forsaken him at the moment when he needed God the most. Jesus Christ endured to the sharpest degree every pain and suffering that we can experience in this life. And he did not deserve any of it. He suffered in our stead, atoning not for sins that he committed, but for the sins we committed.

The Cross, then, is the center of Christian living because it was the center of Christ's own mission in the world. He urges us to follow him on the road of suffering. But only with faith can we heed Christ's command. Rather than deny ourselves, there is a real temptation to exalt ourselves as too wonderful to be forced to endure a given suffering. When we do so, we allow suffering to consume us, to lead us down the road to resentment, bitterness, or despondency.

Christ's suffering was redemptive—it brought about our salvation. Yet he left his mission open so that we, too, may participate in it by uniting our sufferings with his.[24] We can offer our suffering as our prayer for our own redemption and for that of others. This is the meaning behind the old Catholic exhortation to "offer

24. John Paul II, Apostolic Letter on the Christian Meaning of Human Suffering, *Salvifici Doloris* (February 11, 1984), 24. Vatican website: *www.vatican.va*.

up" our sufferings. That is, by a conscious act of the will, we pray along with our pains, asking God to save us and others from sin by them, just as Christ saved us by his sufferings. So for Jesus as for us: there is no Easter glory without the horrors of Good Friday, for however long and to whatever degree God allows for each of us.

To suffer in imitation of Christ is very difficult, and it is likely that we will experience, many times over, both the success of offering up our pains to God in prayer and the failure of wallowing in our own misery. Laden with the Cross, Jesus fell three times on his way to redemption. We are likely to fall far more often as we carry the cross of suffering on our own paths. So long as we seek God's forgiveness for our falls, we can begin the journey again, day after day, year after year, until God calls us to himself.

We never suffer alone. We do so alongside Christ and our fellow Catholics. The present wounds in the body—the sufferings of its members and the harm inflicted upon them by sin—are a source of sadness for Christ its head, even as he reigns eternally in heaven. They all also harm our brothers and sisters in faith, who, because of our real union through baptism, suffer in unison. But this same union allows us to offer our sufferings for the good of our fellow members and for the health of the Church as a whole, as St. Paul has showed us: "I rejoice in my sufferings for your sake, and in my flesh I complete what is lacking in Christ's afflictions for the sake of his body, that is, the Church" (Col 1:24). In this time of acute suffering within the Body of Christ, we can bring about healing by offering up these sufferings for the healing of the whole Church and of those who have been gravely wounded by her leaders and members.

Far from being of secondary importance, the mission of lay men and women is essential to the Church's own mission of spreading the gospel of Christ through our prayer, our work, and even our suffering. As we seek to play our role in the great drama of salvation, we can pray for a proper perspective along with St. John Henry Newman:

> God has created me to do him some definite service; he has committed some work to me which he has not committed to another. I have my mission—I never may know it in this life, but I shall be told it in the next. Somehow I am necessary for his purposes, as necessary in my place as an Archangel in his . . . Yet I have a part in this great work; I am a link in a chain, a bond of connexion between persons. He has not created me for naught. I shall do good, I shall do his work; I shall be an angel of peace, a preacher of truth in my own place, while not

> intending it, if I do but keep his commandments and serve him in my calling.[25]

Between Saints and Sinners

In one of the most moving passages in modern Catholic literature, Lord Marchmain, the apostate father in Evelyn Waugh's *Brideshead Revisited*, after years of living an adulterous relationship in Venice, returns home to England to die. Surrounded by his family, he first refuses the priest summoned to anoint him. Unperturbed, Fr. Mackay speaks beautifully of the power of God's grace, even for the hardest of sinners, at the end of one's life. Sure enough, when Lord Marchmain took his final turn, Fr. Mackay returned and anointed him, finally repentant. Like the good thief on the cross, Lord Marchmain stole heaven in his final moment—not because he deserved it, but because God graciously and mercifully willed it.

Most of us find ourselves somewhere between saints such as More and Molla and characters such as Marchmain. Yet we all are equally part of the Body of Christ.

First, we are all children of God, and the Church is home for each of us. Before God, the greatest saints and fallen away Catholics share an equal dignity: we are loved

---

25. John Henry Newman, *Meditations and Devotions*, ed. W.P. Neville (New York: Longmans, Green, and Co., 1907), 301–302.

as sinners for whom Christ died. Though some Catholics at times may feel alienated from the Church or from their fellow parishioners for any number of reasons—sin, divorce, personal feelings of inadequacy, differences over Church teachings, grievances with the pastor or fellow worshippers—we can never allow these human challenges to undermine the deeper, spiritual union with Christ and one another that exists through baptism.

Second, all Catholics share the call to holiness, to overcome sin and mediocrity. We are too quick to excuse ourselves from this call. Serious religious devotion, saintly living, and self-denial, we rationalize, is for someone else, not for *me*. We are not interested, or we do not want to make the painful changes to our lives that we know God wants. But, in reality, it is we who are closing ourselves off from God because we do not want to change our ways.

Jesus did not seek out the saints of his day. Rather, he sought out ordinary people—sinners with weaknesses, foibles, fears—and built his Church upon them. It was not because of their human talents that the Church rose up, grew, and established herself across the world against seemingly insurmountable odds. No. It was because God worked through the men and women he chose, sanctifying them with his grace and guiding them with his Spirit. These men and women whose names are recorded in the Bible and in history—Mary Magdalene, the twelve apostles, Paul, Zacchaeus, Simon of Cyrene, Ignatius of Antioch, Justin Martyr, Agatha, Perpetua, Felicity—did what St. Peter eventually did: they opened themselves to God's grace and allowed themselves to be changed by it. They turned away from sin and embraced the commandment to love. The love of God then inspired them to build up the Church. If we wish to see the Church recover from her current crisis, we must overcome our reluctance and embrace God's call to sanctity.

Countless examples of mediocre people transformed into saints gives us real hope that we, too, can be transformed. We also know from their experiences that spiritual transformation is a slow and even painful process. So we should not be discouraged if our change is not immediate, or if we lapse back into habits that we thought we had overcome. It is for this reason that the Church exists: to offer us Christ's healing medicine in the sacraments so we can resume our races. And race we must. We know what the Church's wounds are. We have two choices: we can let the wounds consume us so that we look only inward to ourselves with disgust and resentment, or, imitating Christ and the saints, we can offer the suffering we feel from our wounds for our own redemption and for that of our fellow Catholics.

We must open ourselves to surprises sent from God. When God instructed St. Francis of Assisi, "Rebuild my Church," Francis began at once to collect money to repair the dilapidated church of San Damiano. He did not realize that God wanted something much more—to rebuild the whole people of God, who, like today, were suffering from the effects of sin. God's grace is the driving force in all our efforts in pursuit of holiness and in building up the Church, and he often leads us in ways we would never dream of. In the words of fifteenth century monk Thomas à Kempis, "human beings propose, but God disposes."[26] Our task is to discern through prayer where God is leading us at a given moment, and then to make an act of faith that he will help us carry out his will.

We take comfort in knowing that, while our individual vocations and respective tasks may be unique to us, we never carry them out alone. We have the full support of Christ and his Church in all our efforts. Jesus warned the apostles at the last supper, "Apart from me you can do nothing" (Jn 15:5). In addition to God's grace animating our works, we receive the strength we need directly from the Church's sacraments

26. Thomas à Kempis, *The Imitation of Christ*, Book I, Chapter 19, 2 (New York: Catholic Book Publishing Co., 1993), 42.

that fortify our faith and keep us from surrendering. In the end, it is not our efforts but God's grace that enables our tasks to bear fruit: "I planted, Apollos watered, but God gave the growth. So, neither he who plants nor he who waters is anything, but only God who gives the growth" (1 Cor 3:6–7).

If God deems us worthy, our final glorification occurs not in this life, but at our judgments after our deaths. The Church's own glorification also does not occur in this life, when she will always be weighed down by the sin she exists to combat. Jesus' parable of the weeds among the wheat points to this final cleansing of the Church (Mt 13:24–30).

At the end of time, the sin that exists in the Church will be no more. Like the weeds bundled and burned, those who refused to repent of their sins will receive the penalty that they have chosen for themselves: hell, which makes permanent the separation from God that they maintained during their lives. By contrast, those who repented, who asked God for mercy, will be like the wheat, gathered into the barn of heaven, where they will be washed clean in the blood of the Lamb of God. The mystical Body of Christ will be glorified like Christ's physical body. The Church's signs that once made the divine life of God present to the world will be no more, as the reality to which they have been pointing all these centuries will be at hand. The eternal wedding feast of the Lamb, for which the Church has been preparing us our whole lives, will reach its crescendo, as Christ the Bridegroom brings his Bride the Church into the ultimate embrace of eternal union with him.

7

Afterword: To love the Church

Love is an act of the will, a decision that we make to give our best to another. Love is often associated with romance and sweeping emotions, but it need not be. When we take care of a sick family member, lend an ear to a needy friend, or carry out a physically demanding task as a favor, we are performing acts of love that are born not of romantic feelings, but of self-sacrifice.

Love toward our mothers is of this kind. The exuberant love of young children for their mothers eventually ebbs as they reach adolescence; as children begin to assert their independence, they often run into conflict with their mothers' will for them. Occasionally, these conflicts harden and strain the mother-child relationship for years to come. But, more often than not, as children enter adulthood and become parents themselves, their relationships with their mothers become affective again, as they realize that, through all the quarreling, their mothers only wanted what was best for them. Now, as adults, though conscious of their mothers' shortcomings, they are grateful for the love and the countless acts of self-sacrifice that they received from their mothers over so many years. This gratitude then propels them to take care of their aging mothers as they decline in health. Feelings of affection may again wane in the rigors of life's final moments, yet the acts of love, the decisions to sacrifice for their mothers in return for all they have received from them, triumph.

Our relationship with our holy mother the Church is similar. The excitement we might have experienced as young children when we entered a church building, received our First Holy Communion, or celebrated Christmas fades over time. As we age, we become aware of sins committed by our fellow Catholics and by the Church's leaders, actions directly contrary to what they profess. We can be dragged down by this reality and overwhelmed by sin's horrific effects. We can also come into conflict with the Church's teachings as we assert our independence. Our conflicts can harden and prompt us to withdraw from the Church for a time.

As with our natural mothers, we can again have a strong relationship with our spiritual mother. That is, we can love the Church. This love is an act of the will, and it begins when we recall the incredible gift that the

Church has given each of us: communion with Jesus Christ, our savior.

The Incarnation of the Son of God was the definitive event of human history. So definitive that it had to be perpetuated through all subsequent time. The Church is Christ's chosen instrument for keeping him present to all people until he comes again. In the words of third-century bishop St. Cyprian of Carthage, "No one can have God as his Father who does not have the Church as his mother."[1]

The Church gives us the inestimable gift of divine life. As such, she is worthy of our love, our support, and our continued patronage. Through it all, she is, as we saw in Chapter 5, a gift and a blessing.

Loving the Church does not mean that we ignore or discount the sins of Church members, bishops, and priests. Rather, we must work to heal the sin present within her, just as we work to take care of our natural mothers when they become ill. We achieve this, in the first place, through cultivating holiness within ourselves through prayer, frequent reception of the sacraments, acts of sacrifice, and acts of charity. Only then are we

---

1. Cyprian of Carthage, *De Catholicae Ecclesiae Unitate*, 6, quoted in Josemaría Escrivá, *In Love with the Church* (New York: Scepter Publishers, 2007), 58.

prepared to help our fellow members of the Body of Christ, including our priests and bishops. We first have to pray; only then are we spiritually prepared to call out sins, to help our fellow members acknowledge and confess them, and then to establish a firm purpose of amendment never to sin again. These are the four steps that are needed—and have always been needed—to reform the Church. Structures are important, but they are only as effective as the people who live by them. The only sure way to combat sin is with God's grace.

This returns us to the paradoxical state of the Church that is simultaneously divine and human, the storehouse of grace and the refuge of sinners. So long as human beings run the marathon to heaven, there will be failures, sins, and scandals. Just as our natural mothers need us to remain steadfast in our commitment to them when they are ill, so must we remain for our holy mother, the Catholic Church. Though her members may fail, she herself will never fail, for Christ remains at her head, guaranteeing her as his means of salvation, even at the darkest moments of our journeys.

BIBLIOGRAPHY

Magisterial Documents

Congregation for the Doctrine of the Faith. Declaration *Inter Insigniores* on the Question of Admission of Women to the Ministerial Priesthood (October 15, 1976). Vatican website: *www.vatican.va.*

———. *Letter to the Bishops of the Catholic Church on Some Aspects of the Church Understood as Communion* (May 28, 1992). Vatican website: *www.vatican.va.*

Francis. Apostolic Constitution on Ecclesiastical Universities and Faculties, *Veritatis Gaudium* (January 29, 2018). Vatican website: *www.vatican.va.*

———. *Homily on the Solemnity of the Nativity of the Lord.* (December 24, 2019).

John Paul II. Apostolic Letter on Reserving Priestly Ordination to Men Alone, *Ordinatio Sacerdotalis* (May 22, 1994). Vatican website: *www.vatican.va.*

———. Apostolic Exhortation on the Formation of Priests in the Circumstances of the Present Day, *Pastores Dabo Vobis* (March 15, 1992). Vatican website: *www.vatican.va.*

———. Apostolic Letter on the Christian Meaning of Human Suffering, *Salvifici Doloris* (February 11, 1984). Vatican website: *www.vatican.va.*

———. On the Eucharist in its Relationship to the Church, *Ecclesia de Eucharistia* (April 17, 2003). Vatican website: *www.vatican.va.*

———. *Letter to all the Priests on the Occasion of Holy Thursday 1979* (April 8, 1979). Vatican website: *www.vatican.va.*

———. *Letter to Priests on Holy Thursday 2004* (April 6, 2004). Vatican website: *www.vatican.va.*

Constitution on the Sacred Liturgy, *Sacrosanctum Concilium* (December 4, 1963). Vatican website: *www.vatican.va*

Decree on the Ministry and Life of Priests, *Presbyterorum Ordinis* (December 7, 1965). Vatican website: *www.vatican.va.*

Dogmatic Constitution on Divine Revelation, *Dei Verbum* (November 18, 1965). Vatican website: *www.vatican.va.*

Dogmatic Constitution on the Church, *Lumen Gentium* (November 21, 1964). Vatican website: *www.vatican.va.*

Pius XII. Encyclical on the Mystical Body of Christ *Mystici Corporis Christi*, (June 29, 1943). Vatican website: *www.vatican.va.*

General Works

Ancient Christian Commentary on Scripture: Genesis 12–50. Edited by Mark Sheridan. Downers Grove, Illinois: InterVarsity Press, 2002.

Ante-Nicene Fathers, Vol. 1. Edited by Alexander Roberts, James Donaldson, and A. Cleveland Cox. New York: Charles Scriber's Sons, 1903.

Aristotle. *The Basic Works of Aristotle.* Edited by Richard McKeon. New York: Random House, 1941.

Aurelius Augustine. "Questionum in Heptateuchum Libri Septem." In *Patrologiae Cursus Completus. Series Latina*, 34. Edited by J. Migne. Paris, 1843.

Barron, Robert. *Letter to a Suffering Church*. Park Ridge, Illinois: Word on Fire Catholic Ministries, 2019.

Benedict XVI. *Jesus of Nazareth: From the Baptism of the Jordan to the Transfiguration*. Translated by Adrian J. Walker. New York: Doubleday, 2007.

———. "The Church and the Scandal of Sexual Abuse." Catholic News Agency. April 10, 2019.

Bunson, Matthew. *Our Sunday Visitor's Encyclopedia of Catholic History*. Huntington, Indiana: Our Sunday Visitor Publishing Division, 1995.

Catherine of Siena. *St. Catherine of Siena as Seen in her Letters*. Translated and edited by Vida D. Scudder. New York: E.P. Dutton & Co., 1905.

Duggan, Dexter. "St. Gianna's Final Sacrifice Well-Known . . . But What of Her Decades of Faith that Came Before?" *The Wanderer Press*, September 19, 2019.

Dulles, Avery. *Magisterium: Teacher and Guardian of the Faith*. Naples, Florida: Sapientia Press, 2007.

Escrivá, Josemaría. *In Love with the Church*. New York: Scepter Publishers, 2007.

———. *The Way. Furrow. The Forge*. New York: Scepter Publishers, 2011.

Francis of Assisi. *Francis of Assisi—The Saint: Early Documents*, Vol. 1. Edited by Regis J. Armstrong, J.A. Wayne Hellmann, and William J. Short. New York: New City Press, 2002.

Gilson, Étienne. "The Intelligence in the Service of Christ the King." In *Christianity and Philosophy*. New York: Sheed & Ward, 1939.

Griffin, Carter. *Why Celibacy? Reclaiming the Fatherhood of the Priest*. Steubenville, Ohio: Emmaus Road Publishing, 2019.

Kelly, J. N. D. *The Oxford Dictionary of Popes*. New York: Oxford University Press, 1986.

à Kempis, Thomas. *The Imitation of Christ*. New York: Catholic Book Publishing Co., 1993.

Kereszty, Roch. *Jesus Christ: Fundamentals of Christology*, 3rd Edition. New York: Society of St. Paul/Alba House, 2011.

Ignatius of Antioch. *Letter to the Smyrnaeans*. In *The Apostolic Fathers*. Edited by J.B. Lightfoot. Stilwell, Kansas: Digireads.com Publishing, 2007.

Ignatius of Loyola. *The Spiritual Exercises of St. Ignatius*. Translated by Anthony Mottola. New York: Image Books, 1964.

International Theological Commission. *Select Themes of Ecclesiology on the Occasion of the Twentieth Anniversary of the Closing of the Second Vatican Council*. 1984. Vatican website: *www.vatican.va*.

Introduction to Catholicism, 2nd ed. Edited by Jeffrey Cole. Downers Grove, Illinois: Midwest Theological Forum, 2018.

de Lubac, Henri. *The Splendor of the Church*. Translated by Michael Mason. San Francisco: Ignatius Press, 1999.

Monti, James. *The King's Good Servant But God's First*. San Francisco: Ignatius Press, 1997.

Newman, John Henry. *An Essay on the Development of Christian Doctrine*. Notre Dame, Indiana: University of Notre Dame Press, 1989.

———. *Apologia Pro Vita Sua*. New York: Penguin Classics, 1994.

———. *Fifteen Sermons Preached before the University of Oxford between A.D. 1826 and 1843*, 3rd ed. Notre Dame, Indiana: University of Notre Dame Press, 1997.

———. *Meditations and Devotions*. Edited. by W.P. Neville. New York: Longmans, Green, and Co., 1907.

Nicene and Post-Nicene Fathers, Second Series, Vol. 11. Edited by Philip Schaff and Henry Wace. Translated by C. A. Heurtley. Buffalo, New York: Christian Literature Publishing Company, 1894.

O'Neel, Brian. *39 New Saints You Should Know*. Cincinnati: Servant Books, 2010.

O'Neill, Colman. *Meeting Christ in the Sacraments*. Revised by Romanus Cessario. New York: Society of St. Paul/Alba House, 1991.

Pieper, Josef. *Faith, Hope, Love*. San Francisco: Ignatius Press, 1997.

Ratzinger, Joseph. *Introduction to Christianity*. Translated by J.R. Foster. San Francisco: Ignatius Press, 2004.

———. *Milestones: Memoirs 1927–1977*. Translated by Erasmo Leiva-Merikakis. San Francisco: Ignatius Press, 1998.

———. "The Question of the Concept of Tradition: A Provisional Response." *God's Word: Scripture, Tradition, Office*. Edited by Peter Hünermann and Thomas Söding. Translated by Henry Taylor. San Francisco: Ignatius Press, 2008.

Reynolds, E.E. *The Field Is Won: The Life and Death of Saint Thomas More*. Milwaukee: The Bruce Publishing Company, 1968.

Sullins, D. Paul. D. "Is Catholic clergy sex abuse related to homosexual priests?" Lake Charles, Louisiana: The Ruth Institute, 2018.

Thomas Aquinas. *Summa Theologica*. Translated by the Fathers of the English Dominican Province. New York: Benziger Brothers, Inc., 1947.

Vianney, John. *The Little Catechism of The Curé of Ars*. Rockford, Illinois: TAN Books and Publishers, Inc., 1987.